CW01024059

50 SENTENCES THAT MAKE LIFE EASIER

www.penguin.co.uk

KARIN KUSCHIK

50 SENTENCES THAT MAKE LIFE EASIER

A GUIDE FOR MORE SELF-CONFIDENCE

Translated by Benjamin Posener

bantam

TRANSWORLD PUBLISHERS
Penguin Random House, One Embassy Gardens,
8 Viaduct Gardens, London SW11 7BW
www.penguin.co.uk

Transworld is part of the Penguin Random House group of companies
whose addresses can be found at global.penguinrandomhouse.com

First published by Rowohlt Taschenbuch Verlag 2022
First published in Great Britain in 2025 by Bantam
an imprint of Transworld Publishers

Copyright © Karin Kuschik 2022
English translation © Benjamin Posener 2025

A CIP catalogue record for this book
is available from the British Library.

ISBN 9780857507037

Typeset in 11.25/15pt Wolpe Pegasus by Jouve (UK), Milton Keynes.
Printed and bound in Great Britain by Clays Ltd, Elcograf S.p.A.

The authorized representative in the EEA is Penguin Random House Ireland,
Morrison Chambers, 32 Nassau Street, Dublin D02 YH68.

To all my clients. And to my friends who have often enquired, with benevolent stubbornness, as to where they might find the trove with all my humble treasures.

Here it is, my friends, here it is.

Contents

Prologue

Dear reader, this book will save you time. Time you might otherwise waste in misunderstandings, righteous indignation or pointless self-monologues – things that lead you astray and turn your life into a drama. The alternative I'm offering: small sentences with big impacts. Sentences that make life easier. Each one is an invitation, an appeal for more honesty, clarity, self-leadership and authenticity.

Even if you adopt only, say, five of these fifty sentences and integrate them into your everyday vocabulary, they will most probably change your life – transforming both the impression you make on others and how you regard yourself.

Some of the things I propose might sound outrageously irreverent or liberating, others perhaps unspectacular or even banal. That's intended. I'd like you to feel like it's a breeze, simple to apply yet compellingly effective. What could be better? After all, the idea is to make your life easier.

If you're interested in clarity, setting boundaries and experiencing appreciation, this book will be particularly valuable for you; the thousands of coaching sessions I've conducted have shown me that most issues have their roots here. No matter what subject a client approached me about, in the end it boiled down to one of these themes, often all three combined.

It follows that all the stories in this book are linked to these topics, and a key term here is *self-leadership*. If you are interested in growing as a person, you'll intuitively veer towards the topic of leadership conduct: how do I lead the members in my team? How do I conduct my relationships, my marriage? How do I lead a conversation? Indeed, how do I lead myself? I can tell you for certain: self-leadership is the prerequisite for less ego and a greater sense of responsibility for articulating what you need – thus it forms the basis for experiencing wonderful, intricate feelings of happiness, irrespective of the situation.

Have you noticed that there are many giants of knowledge who turn into dwarfs when it comes to applying what they know? It's a tragic combination – unnecessary and sad, all at once. That's why I've always offered shortcuts that enable you to apply the knowledge you have gained quickly, effectively, and in a relaxed way. People who have a stock of such dependable sentences in their arsenal, for when they're needed, feel much more confident. And the relaxed assuredness that comes with this opens up a world of possibilities.

I love telling stories and I'm also a big fan of citing examples. So, these chapters are real stories: about how each sentence was born, the situation in which it proved invaluable, or whose life became easier by using it. They're all true. And then again, they're not – because I've invented the names of the protagonists, swapped the names of cities, places and businesses. You could call the result a true-life cocktail in which even the people the stories are based on would not be able to recognize themselves. Discretion has been a top priority.

You can read this book in any order you like. It's not chronological and each chapter is self-contained. So, you could dive in wherever you like. Some may wish to consult the contents list first to see which sentence particularly appeals to them. Others may find these suggestions irritating and do what they always do: start at the beginning and finish at the end – it's a book, for heaven's sake! But to my mind, it's also a treasure chest offering concrete solutions for specific situations. That's why I think it important to emphasize that you can be selective. Zoom in on the chapter that sounds like it might be just right for that challenging meeting tomorrow. That way, you can try it out the very next day. Or you can let chance decide: open it anywhere, and away you go. This is the age of finger food, so I'm serving up bite-sized delicacies. Each titbit can be consumed in under ten minutes. You can insert a sentence in a conversation or you can direct it as an inward message to yourself – some actually work best that way.

And now, enjoy the book! I'll be very happy if you experience some magical moments. Welcome to my world.

1

I DECIDE WHO PUSHES MY BUTTONS

The atmosphere in the Berlin recording studio is frantic. The manager of a well-known folk singer is shouting at the producer and he's barking back at him. The singer herself appears completely relaxed, sipping her latte. I'm there as the lyricist, and when I ask her how she manages to stay so calm in the midst of all the chaos, she just shrugs and says: 'I decide who pushes my buttons.' Wow, what a great line! It's *me* who decides?! I immediately resolve to add this sentence to my list of magic mantras. And since then, it's made my life easier – and those of hundreds of my clients – in wondrous ways.

'The annoying thing about anger is: it's bad for you, without doing anyone else any good either,' the journalist and author Kurt Tucholsky is quoted as saying. That's a good way to put it because anger is a totally superfluous emotion that doesn't lead anywhere, it just makes you even angrier. In the same way that joy breeds joy and doubts breed more doubts, anger feeds on anger. Getting angry simply doesn't cut it. But try telling that to someone who's on the verge of going ballistic because they feel slighted or threatened and they're taking everything personally. They're unlikely to say: 'Hey, great advice! I'll stop being angry at once. Thanks for the tip!'

It's a fact that rational reflection, awareness of the facts or empathy rarely lead to changes in behaviour. Such shifts are always the result of a change in attitude. And that's why my first tip for you is so powerful: it's not about deploying a rhetorical tool, it's about an inner shift in perspective and attitude. But how do we get there? Or, rather, *when* do we get there? The answer is: when our rational understanding of a situation also touches us on the emotional level; when whatever irks us makes us feel that we absolutely want to experience something totally different. Because it's only when we are sufficiently motivated that we make a concrete decision – from then on, a lot of things become much easier.

I grew up in Frankfurt, so I'm familiar with the phrase 'Before I get angry I'd rather not care'. That's pretty sound advice because – apart from revealing a certain smugness that's typical for the region – it's an expression of a particular mindset: being self-determined. In essence, it describes an attitude where challenges are taken seriously, but not so seriously as to give others power over how we feel. Why on earth would we do that, especially if the person is doing his or her utmost to annoy us? Why would you want someone else to be able to decide how you feel, or cause you to lie awake at night, worrying? Or prompt you to write dozens of vengeful emails in your mind?

All these things are senseless. They ruin your mood and

steal valuable time that you could be using to enjoy your life. And yet, incredibly, they happen all the time. If you could feed the energy people on earth expend on getting upset into the electricity grid, you could probably generate enough power to illuminate entire cities – for ever. And the fact is, everything we have to deal with becomes twice as taxing when anger is involved, and even more so when we get angry about being angry. So, let's at least not contribute to this sorry state of affairs.

But isn't that easier said than done? Doesn't it depend on your personality? No. The only thing it depends on is reaching a decision. So, if you're someone who values self-determination, freedom and taking responsibility, this chapter will enrich your life. And it will be easier to put into practice than you might think. To be clear: it's an illusion to think that circumstances determine how you feel. In reality, the way you feel is and always has been the result of how you, in your very own way, react to those circumstances. If you firmly resolve that from this point on you will decide who or what angers you, you'll find that you have made a huge step in the right direction.

Make a deal with yourself, so that your new mantra – 'I decide who pushes my buttons' – becomes a part of your mental soundtrack, part of who you are. Because, if it all makes sense to you today but it's just a fading memory tomorrow, it's not going to work. Just make the decision that when a situation next arises that might make you angry, you won't immediately react. Instead, just breathe out for a moment. And when you inhale again, remember the mantra and decide if you want to get angry. If you're

confronted by someone, and you don't feel like react-
ing with anger, a response could be: 'There's lots I could
say to that, but I'd rather stick to the topic. Is that OK with
you?' Or: 'I don't feel like getting annoyed, it's a waste of
time. Let's stick to the subject, all right?' Or perhaps: 'I
hear you, but how do we move forward from here? I suggest we take a constructive approach.'

But it really isn't that important exactly what you say. I'm
convinced that it's never about finding the next brilliant
retort, even if most of my clients resolutely stick to this
theory. If your attitude is positive – let's say, you're self-
possessed and that's where you want to be – it's irrelevant
how eloquent or casual your response is. You could just as
easily say nothing. If, instead, you're consumed by a feeling
of inner restlessness and irritation, then even the most brilliant retort won't lead to a satisfactory solution.

And if your 'adversary' feels provoked by your level-
headedness? If they say something like: 'Aren't you at least
going to hit back?' Or: 'Why aren't you losing your temper
too?' Well, you can just lean back, casually inspect your
fingernails and say: 'I decide who pushes my buttons.'

WHAT THIS SENTENCE GIVES YOU
SELF-ASSUREDNESS
A CLEAR CONSCIENCE
SAVES YOU TIME

2

THIS ISN'T AGAINST YOU, IT'S FOR ME

Katja is fuming. She throws her bag on to the yellow chair next to her and immediately blurts out: 'I have to let off steam, it's about last night!' She tells me about her chaotic and exhausting day at work and how all she'd wanted to do for hours was get home and have a nice long, relaxing bath. But it also happened to be the day her boyfriend had finally made the effort to get tickets for the cinema that evening. Tom never takes the initiative, and she's complained about it on many occasions. A touchy situation.

Katja was determined; she was set on her plan: 'That's a real shame, but right now I just want a hot bath. I'm not up for anything else tonight.'

Tom: 'What?! You can have a bath any day and I've already paid for the tickets!' And the next thing he heard was her turning on the taps. He entered the bathroom and saw Katja pouring blue bath salts into the water.

'Oh great, now you're trying to make me feel bad about it!' Katja almost yelled, her voice drowned out by the sound of the gushing water. She was struggling not to cry.

Tom: 'Me, making you feel bad? You're the one who's just ruined the evening! So, this is what happens when I try to surprise you!' He stalked out of the bathroom, slamming the door.

You're probably familiar with these kinds of accusations: 'When you're like this, it makes me feel really bad' or 'I feel awful and it's your fault.' Sure, in the heat of the moment we might actually think that's true – feelings don't lie. But later, when we've calmed down, we ought to realize that it's actually impossible: how exactly could someone else determine what we feel? Don't we have a say in the matter? In fact, aren't we in charge? In truth, aren't we the ones who create our own feelings?

If these sound to you like leading questions, it's because they are. As a coach, I'm naturally convinced that it's always us who decide how we feel – you could say it comes with the territory. Do you agree? Or does this statement make you feel a bit queasy? Our willingness to accept something is closely related to our stress-tolerance and our experiences – which, of course, determine the way we view the world, and where we stand in terms of self-esteem and empowerment. Remember the first sentence in this book: 'I decide who pushes my buttons.' That would also fit here.

But I'd like to suggest a different one for our disastrous hot-bath-cancelled-movie drama, similarly effective and more analytical: 'This isn't *against* you, it's *for* me.' An important distinction. One that enables us to draw a clear boundary between ourselves and others. A boundary which is, unfortunately, often forgotten – resulting in intrusive behaviour.

When this happens, we're wading into the murky waters of insinuation. And once we're there, me and you, intention and result, truth and perception get mixed up and confused. In this situation it becomes almost impossible to separate one*self* from the *other*.

'Shall we go and see a film?'

'I'd rather stay at home.'

'Now you've ruined my evening!'

That exchange (condensed) is one way to experience an evening. Here's an alternative.

Tom: 'Fancy going to see a film?'

Katja: 'Oh, what a shame, I'm just not up for it this evening. I'm completely exhausted and I've been dying to have a relaxing bath all day.'

Tom: 'Oh great, I've finally bought some tickets and now—'

Katja: 'That's really a shame, I'm so sorry. This is what I really need to do at the moment. But thanks for the lovely idea.'

Tom: 'Are you really going to do this to me?'

Katja: 'I'm not doing anything to you. This isn't *against you*, it's *for me*. That's a big difference.'

That's how it could have been. And if Tom then still insists on feeling he's been slighted, so be it. Getting het-up is a choice. And Katja doesn't have to feel guilty. That, too, is a matter of choice.

Try to be clear about this as often as you can: there's a big difference between someone deciding something that's *against* you or *for* themselves. It's worthwhile considering this briefly before crossing swords. You can neatly circumvent a lot of unnecessary conflicts you might have with others or, depending on your temperament, with yourself.

'This isn't against you, it's for me' is a sentence for people on both sides of a statement: for those who wish to *say* it to gracefully draw a line, and for those who get the opportunity to *hear* the statement delivered in this way. In my experience, the idea that a statement needn't be *against* someone is particularly valuable for people who in the past may have tended to take everything personally.

If this is a sentence that appeals to you, and you feel it might free up energy you'd rather invest more gainfully, you might like to go straight to sentences 17 or 42: 'I think this issue is yours' and 'I won't take it personally' – these sentences also deal with the art of establishing boundaries more easily. They have a similar liberating effect as the sentence Katja has successfully deployed on many occasions since her hot-bath quarrel.

And if it's the other way round, and you're the one feeling attacked? Then imagine the other person has just explained that their decision has nothing to do with you, that their credo is simply 'This isn't against you, it's for me'. You'll probably find you can be much more relaxed about the whole thing.

WHAT THIS SENTENCE GIVES YOU

CLARITY

UNDERSTANDING

HARMONY

I APOLOGIZE

Life would be so much easier if everyone used these three essential words listed in their own language for tourists in every travel guide: Thanks. Please. Sorry. Even people who are reluctant to speak the language of the country they are visiting usually manage at least a semblance of these three words. But in their own language, they seem to disappear in the vortex of everyday life.

The other day in a supermarket. A man studying his shopping list while pushing his trolley in the general direction of the checkout rams it into the Achilles tendon of a woman standing at the back of the queue. She cries out in pain. Shocked, the man pulls his trolley back a little while the woman rubs her calf. He says: 'What? I'm wearing my reading glasses!' Observing people while they're shopping can be a treat for behavioural psychologists.

At the recycling point in the same supermarket I witness an exchange I've often heard and which never ceases to amaze me. A woman who has obviously changed her mind about returning her bottles takes a few steps backwards and bumps into another woman. The bottle lady says: 'Oops!' The other woman: 'Watch where you're going!' Bottle lady: 'I don't have eyes in the back of my head, do I?!' Can't argue with that – which is why it might be an idea to turn one's head before marching backwards.

The victim-reversal response is so abstruse, it's almost comical. But why is the urge to justify oneself stronger than the wish to apologize? Shouldn't it be the other way round? It certainly doesn't seem to be programmed into our DNA. In some people, as I realized recently, the option of apologizing – as a prioritized response in such situations – simply doesn't exist.

To some extent, our childhood experiences in this regard play a role. For example, the other day I saw a mother in a playground shouting at her son: 'You're going to apologize to that boy, right now! That's not how we behave. Go on, say you're sorry and make it right!' When the boy reluctantly obeyed, gaze directed at the ground, the mother added: 'Look him in the eye and say it like you mean it!' Well, that's a form of education, I suppose: drumming it in, rather than explaining. And reflecting on this, perhaps I can better understand why the man with the reading glasses couldn't just say: 'Oh, I'm sorry! Did it hurt? I apologize.'

You can only speak a language if you've learnt it. Nevertheless, I've always thought it a bit feeble to blame one's failings as an adult on one's childhood. Nobody taught us how to apologize? That's a shame. So, let's teach ourselves now – should be possible, given our innate capacity to learn things. *It's Never Too Late to Have a Happy Childhood* – Ben Furman's book of that title comes to mind. It always makes me feel optimistic and reassured. Its message, in a nutshell: we always have a choice.

If you're someone who finds it difficult to apologize, you might be motivated by the realization that it's often you who is the main beneficiary of the apology. The term stems from the Greek word *apologia* – to speak or write in defence of something. You could say we're explaining our behaviour to relieve ourselves of a burden. Nitpickers might object that apology is impossible: it's up to others to forgive us. That's true. And yet the word 'apology' (or 'sorry') is part of most people's common vocabulary. So, let's stick with it. Because whether you're a 'May I apologize?' or a 'Can you forgive me?' person, both expressions provide us with a sense of relief. We're demonstrating acceptance, remorse and, if required, a willingness to undo the damage. So, let's use the word 'apologize' more often. And by the same token, let us as recipients of an apology simply accept it rather than brushing it off with a remark like 'No worries!'

Some people take a roundabout route to express their regret, buying flowers or expensive jewellery, accompanied by an embarrassed remark such as 'For yesterday . . .' Better than nothing, of course, and such presents can no doubt be endearing. But nothing is better for clearing one's conscience than swallowing one's 'pride' and finding appropriate words to say to someone.

A client of mine, let's call her Ute, used to be inundated with these apology-substitutes. And that phrase 'For yesterday . . .' would have almost been an eloquent offering in the case of her husband who, having lost his temper yet again, would simply mumble: 'You know what that's for . . .' Ute eventually left him and never returned. She also left all the rings, bracelets and necklaces behind.

I'm not suggesting you instantly pack your bags just because your partner can't seem to overcome an inner hurdle. So, what should we do in situations where we're hurt, feel unjustly treated and find ourselves waiting for an apology that simply never comes? For that can quickly happen when someone lacks understanding or is simply too obstinate or too afraid to admit to a mistake. The absence of an apology drives some people mad. So, then what?

Here's my idea. Let the following sentence really sink in. Its power lies in its capacity to pacify that nagging sense of injustice: 'Life becomes easier when we accept an apology we never received.' Life becomes easier still if we can accept we are responsible for our own lives – and just say 'I apologize' a little more often.

WHAT THIS SENTENCE GIVES YOU
PEACE OF MIND
CLARITY
A CLEAR CONSCIENCE

I APOLOGIZE

4

I'D RATHER NOT PROMISE YOU THAT

The view over the evening skyline in Berlin is breathtaking. Illuminated domes, late eighteenth-century villas, church spires, chic rooftop gardens, and in the last afterglow of sunset the high rise on Alexanderplatz. Right before me, almost like an apparition, the Fernsehturm (television tower) shines brightly through the floor-to-ceiling windows. I almost feel like I'm hovering in the sky.

'How lovely to see you! Let the games begin!' David hollers from across the room while his latest flame, Julian, hands me a glass of champagne. 'Great to finally meet you!' he says. He taps his mobile and the melancholy sound of Cigarettes After Sex flows from the speakers. 'Are you expecting someone from *Ideal Home* magazine?' I tease David, who is preparing something in the exquisitely designed kitchen, which seamlessly connects to a dream of a living room. 'Care for a tour of the palace?' asks Julian, who owns it. A promising start to the evening.

After the usual table chatter with the other guests, most of whom I've never met before, and deep into the mellow post-dinner ambience, Julian suddenly proclaims: 'Just imagine, yesterday I asked David if he'd move in with me into the island house and he said yes! We're moving to Majorca!' Applause, congratulations and the clinking of glasses all round. And I cast a sceptical glance at David – which the other guests will hopefully take for a smile. It sends the message: 'Whaaaaat?!' He's got himself into one of his quandaries. He'll never move to Majorca. I've known this free spirit for too long to believe he would do that. He probably just agreed in a flight of romantic fancy. But how will he wiggle himself out of it?

'Don't say yes, when you want to say no.' For years, a poster with this proverb hung in an acquaintance's flat. One day, the poster was gone and Sandra started using a phrase I hadn't heard from her before. 'I'd rather not promise you that, Karin. I'm still unsure about it.' What was that? Sandra was famous for making rash promises she'd conveniently forget about. And now, 'I'd rather not promise you that'? This was definitely a first in our friendship, and a big improvement as far as I was concerned. As someone who takes words seriously and takes people *at their word*, I often end up disappointed when I realize that statements which to my mind are iron-clad are in fact inconsequential chatter. That for some people 'yes' actually means 'no' (or perhaps more accurately 'I don't know') was something that wouldn't have even crossed my mind. It took me a while to reluctantly understand that people who are unreliable – whose behaviour I would deem to be erratic or even irresponsible – would quite keenly describe themselves as 'flexible'. They'd tersely brush me off with an 'I didn't mean it that way', and then I'd be thinking: 'Well, don't *say* something you don't mean!' We all tick differently and it's beneficial to realize this as early as possible.

If you recognize this trait in yourself and would like to get rid of it, it might be a good idea to use a more non-committal phrase. For instance: 'I'd rather not promise you that.' It is especially useful for those of us who would like to be seen to be up for everything, but are just making conversation. Because every time you *don't* use this sentence, the likelihood of creating a problem for yourself and others increases.

It helps to be aware of what we want to promise a person and what we would rather not. After all, you can't know who will take your words at face value, who might presume you are just thinking out loud, and who will have forgotten the whole thing by the next day. Too many pleasant conversations have turned sour over a remark like 'I was only saying!' And in some instances it can ruin an evening, a day or even a holiday.

I once gave a business workshop the title 'More Understanding for Misunderstandings'. It had a lot of insightful moments – for me, too. I was surprised by how quickly it became clear that the topic of *agreements* is a veritable minefield – not necessarily as far as work is concerned, where people tend to be extremely reliable and stick to what has been agreed, but in people's private lives. An interesting phenomenon. Does that ring a bell? Committed at work, negligent at home. That seems quite illogical, on the face of it, since abilities (or personal qualities) aren't suddenly unlearnt. If you can ride a bike, it's not as if that skill is only available on Tuesday afternoons and on the last Saturday of each month. What I'm saying is: if you can stick to deadlines in the office, why not at weekends? How is it possible to be a reliable colleague and then to shed that attribute when you're dealing with your kids? It should actually be a logical impossibility – but you know what it's like with statements that include the word *actually*.

The answer, quite simply, is that many people – especially those who are required to be high performers at work – often feel overwhelmed and want to let their hair down when they get home. They want to re-energize, let themselves drift, and are happy not to have to function efficiently for a change. High performers are often unaware that this desire can strike family members as callous and unappreciative, because they are conscious of their abilities and that blinds them to their shortcomings. And, of course, all this enhances the potential for domestic conflicts.

We can avoid such conflicts by taking a moment before responding in situations which require a commitment. First, listen into yourself. Do you really want to commit? Are you even able to keep that pledge? Do you want to make this promise? If the answer is 'no' or 'I'm not sure', it means you shouldn't say yes. I know this statement may sound banal, but many people don't adhere to this advice. It's that giant-in-knowledge versus dwarf-in-application phenomenon. And sometimes empathy plays a role, too. Because we don't wish to disappoint others we'll promise things we doubt we'll be able, or even know we won't be able, to deliver. Consequently, we end up in exactly the place we intended to avoid at all costs: where we are a disappointment to others. Because, as a result of this behaviour, we'll end up having to cancel something we never should have committed to. A lot of effort for something that could so easily have been avoided.

'I'd rather not promise you that.' This sentence would have been a perfect option for David so as to avoid his Majorca dilemma, no matter how romantic the circumstances. By the way, just to finish that story, David never did move to Majorca – nor even into Julian's breathtaking Berlin apartment. Commitments just aren't his thing, skyline panorama or not. Yet it took him two years and endless debates before he clearly said so. If he had committed himself to being honest, instead of promising his partner something that sounded great for a moment and then felt wrong forever after, he could have spared both of them this emotional roller-coaster ride.

'I'd rather not promise you that' is a good sentence to fall back on when the need arises. It saves us a lot of strife, bumpy detours and disappointment.

WHAT THIS SENTENCE GIVES YOU
HARMONY
CLARITY
SAVES YOU TIME

'**A** new broom sweeps clean!' is the surprising greeting I receive from the newly appointed CEO of a pharmaceuticals company. Brimming with confidence, he's beaming as he marches towards me with open arms in a venue that seems surprisingly big for such a small cinema. This is where his stage training will take place. In two days, he'll be giving his inaugural speech, presenting his vision for the future in front of the company's executives.

'It sounds like you're planning big changes,' I reply. 'Jumping in at the deep end, are you?' I beam back at him, curious as to what the day will bring – especially since today I'm stepping in for his regular coach. Not an easy task.

'Nonsense,' Mr Warncke retorts. 'I'm well prepared, so let's get started.'

I soon realize we've got plenty of work to do. The first line of his planned speech is a catastrophe: 'We *must* improve or our ship will sink!' Wasn't it supposed to be a motivational speech?

Must. Not the neatest word when you're trying to woo your employees. No one is likely to cry out: 'At last! I can't wait to have to must!'

Mr Warncke, however, has no intention of changing his introduction. He hasn't come here to sit in the red armchair and re-type his speech on his laptop. He's here to shine in the limelight. I don't blame him for feeling that way, yet we're stuck with each other. So, I pose the rhetorical question: 'Would you like your audience to be enthralled?'

'You've got an hour,' he grumbles. Too little time to expand on the proverb 'Wanting to is like having to, except of your own free will'. However, I'll gladly do so here.

Having to do something always involves pressure or coercion. You can't do what you'd like; your boss tells you that his or her hands are tied. Yet, people who shape things don't *have to* do them. They *choose* to.

An hour later this realization is reflected in his speech. He's sounding more self-determined and clear, which also provides the space for humour. The hour he grudgingly conceded becomes the rest of the day. And at the end of it, a satisfied CEO even gets some real-life feedback: the camera operator spontaneously claps. Now Mr Warncke knows how good it can feel to captivate an audience using substantive and authentic language. Goosebumps never lie.

Studies have shown that modal verbs like *must* cause stress. Blood pressure, stress hormones, cholesterol – all go up. Added to which, people who are stressed also express themselves that way: 'I must finish writing that offer', 'We must commit', 'Hurry up, I have to leave'. When we're in a must-do spiral, we're not even aware we're increasing our stress level simply by being in that frame of mind. If you are told a hundred times that you *must* do something, as the pressure mounts you'll add a hundred *musts* of your own. It becomes a vicious circle. It's like wearing a quilted jacket and turning up the heating when you're already sweating, rather than shutting it down and opening the windows. What must-doers really can benefit from is a U-turn to a self-determined state of choice.

I recall an interesting exchange in a workshop I once enrolled in, where the topic was 'having to versus wanting to'. A lively young woman explains that she's stressed at work because she must meet a deadline. 'It's not as if I can simply ignore it and not hand in the offer!' she exclaims.

'Why not?' the coach calmly enquires.

Astonished, she replies: 'Because I promised to!'

'Why did you do that?'

'Because I really want that commission.'

'So, you want to get the commission, but you don't want to have to do anything to get it?'

'No!'

'Yes,' the coach insists, maintaining a friendly tone. 'Focus on the word *want*. What you call must, or having to, is the price for achieving what you want.'

I was pretty impressed.

Same workshop, later on: 'You act as if we all had a choice!' a man in his mid-fifties complains. He's wearing an elegant suit and lounging on one of the few available chairs, while most of us are planted on our yoga mats.

'Don't we have choices?' the coach wants to know.

'Of course not! If I don't do my job properly, I'll get the sack.'

'And then?'

'Well, then . . .' The man searches for the right words. 'Then I'm unemployed!'

'And then?' the coach repeats, still in a friendly manner.

'Then I certainly won't be able to pay the mortgage or send the kids to boarding school. All that costs money, you know?'

'Who wanted your children to go to boarding school?'

'We did, of course – it's an opportunity for them!'

'Aha. So, you *want* all that: the house, the school, the job. That's quite a lot of wanting there. And if something doesn't suit you along the way, it suddenly becomes a case of *having to*?'

The elegant-suit man becomes pensive. Again, I was impressed with the coach's reasoning. More than that: I was twenty-three at the time and thought, 'My eyes have been opened! I see everything clearly now!' How sweet.

Yet to this day it's my definition for *having to* do things: 'I want something, but I'm not willing to pay the price for it.' It's worthwhile occasionally applying this insight to those must-do impulses. It helps us see where we really stand. An example: 'I must do my taxes.' Maybe a more accurate statement would be: 'I want to save the money a tax adviser would cost me.' And if you don't have the money for a tax adviser, might this statement be true: 'I'd rather spend my money on something else.' You could endlessly extend this exercise. Having to do something is seldom the case in our part of the world (meaning in wealthy countries). It just often feels that way. Of course, there are exceptions. Rarely, a person might be forced into a course of action that does not relate in any way to any previous desire or action on their part – for example, if there is a miscarriage of justice and the convicted person really *has to* go to prison. For other prisoners it might be more accurate to say: 'I *wanted* to rob a bank.'

Having to is how *wanting* to be free of responsibility often disguises itself. Life becomes easier when we clearly distinguish between coercion and choice.

The philosopher Immanuel Kant said: 'I can, because I want to do what I have to do.' This motivational approach can be very beneficial, especially when it comes to the things we dislike. Bookkeeping, for example. Many even loathe the word. Me too. Then I decided to change my attitude. I was fed up with *having to* sort and categorize every little receipt. So, I thought: 'If I'm going to do bookkeeping, I'll do it on my terms.' Now, I launch my Peaceful Piano playlist, pour lemongrass oil into the aroma diffuser and brew a pot of my favourite tea. That's the only way it makes sense. My credo: before you *have to* do something, you might just as well decide to *want* to do it. Freedom is simply more enjoyable.

When I'm coaching I sometimes recommend – as home-work, so to speak – that my clients reflect on any sentences that start with 'I must' and 'I can't'. This brings clarity and surprising insights. Often, these sentiments are simply not true. They stem from negative ideas and old thoughts. They trigger feelings of compulsion, neediness and self-deprecation. 'Don't believe everything you hear, especially if it's coming from yourself' can be a liberating formula here.

To be clear: *having to* is not an expression I want to put on some blacklist. I haven't banned it from my life. On the contrary, it's like a screaming-red pop-up warning which says: 'You're under a lot of pressure right now!' There's nothing wrong with using these words, as long as you also hear the message that you can only do something about pressure if you're aware of its influence. It's totally normal for our inner guard dog to start barking as soon as words like *having to* drive us into a frenzy. This enables us to pull the emergency brake and to ask ourselves what would do us good. A pause? Having a meal? Cancelling a meeting, taking a deep breath, apologizing, or doing something that's fun, so we can have a good laugh? Because if you're telling yourself and others that you *have to* do everything – i.e. things you don't *want* to do – you are losing your capacity for self-determination. 'Wanting to is like having to, except of your own free will.' Therein lies the subtle, yet important, difference.

*

So, if you want to feel freer – and perhaps even enthral an audience – it's a good idea to abandon the *Titanic* metaphors and be attentive to the bark of the guard dog.

WHAT THIS SENTENCE GIVES YOU
SELF-DETERMINATION
FREEDOM
RELAXATION

6

I DON'T THINK THAT'S REALLY MY DEPARTMENT

Mila is the perfect personal assistant. She personifies that finely attuned skill-set of always being one step ahead, supportive, clear, charming, on-topic, understanding, strategically adept, and clever as well. She has mastered the tightrope act of being indispensable without drawing too much attention to herself. What she's not yet so good at is setting boundaries. In fact she's useless at it, and this is a problem. A problem for her boss, who never knows what to do when he finds her in tears, and a problem for Mila, who – as I discover during our first session – reacts to the concept like a bull to a red rag. She doesn't believe she can change her behaviour without sacrificing who she is. 'Boundaries?! But the team relies on me!' She sounds like she's warding off an attack. 'I'm not the type for that, I can't afford to be!'

Fear is a common reaction from people who have never learnt to draw a line when others go too far. Just the term *boundary* can trigger a hefty reaction. And yet, in my experience, this has for years been one of the major topics when people seek coaching. In fact, I'd go so far as to say it's the most frequent topic, irrespective of where someone works within a hierarchy and how intimate (or intimidating) the issue might be. So, I'm all the more delighted to witness how quickly many clients feel able to change their perspective because they are willing – with a mixture of curiosity and healthy scepticism – to trust in something I experience every day: that it absolutely is possible to set boundaries and still remain charming. You can say 'no' without being labelled a pig. Because that is really the main fear for people who aren't sure whether setting boundaries is a good idea. They don't want to appear to be acting like a pig. I think pigs are lovely animals, by the way. But sticking with the popular slur, that's how drastically some people describe the horrid end of their either/or scale. On the one hand, it says: nice, popular, sympathetic. And on the other, it says: PIG! All that wonderful space, the potential variants in between, has not yet been discovered by those who shy away from setting boundaries. And contemplating the nice-versus-pig scale, it's understandable that most people would prefer to be on the 'nice' side.

This is where (I like to say) maths comes into play. If you equate setting boundaries with being hard, dismissive and bossy, and regard yourself as sympathetic and nice, it's clear why you'd want to steer clear of the topic. So, the first thing that's required is not a change in behaviour, but rather adopting a new equation in your mind. The formula 'setting boundaries = being bossy and tough' is simply counter-productive. Whereas 'I find it easy to be self-assured, clear and charming' can work wonders.

One of the main drivers of stress in transactional analysis is 'to want to please everyone'. If this principle is firmly ingrained in your system, often without you realizing it, you're in a real quandary because the *everyone* in that sentence includes yourself. And pleasing everyone then often requires you to be the last in line – that's if you don't forget yourself completely. Tragically, in this set-up, the one person who can never really be satisfied is you. When we feel driven in this way, it's hard to be successful. So, what's the solution?

A neat little first-aid measure is to start transmitting I-messages. These are those inconspicuous sentences that mention only you. There's nothing in there about the person you're addressing. And because that's the case, no one can feel attacked. This book is packed with I-messages, and one of them is perfect for setting boundaries. Especially when you say it as if it was the most natural thing in the world: 'I don't think that's really my department.' It worked wonders for Mila.

A video conference during Covid. Eight tile-sized faces are displayed on the screen: Mila, as the management assistant, and the seven senior heads of department. Also in view, of course, are the obligatory bookshelves in the background and – I'll never understand why this has to be – too many nose cavities. If only we could agree that up-angle camera shots can be unflattering. But I digress. The meeting takes an hour, during which topics are tossed back and forth, questions are asked and strategies discussed. At the end of the meeting, for which Mila has been taking notes, the social media manager nonchalantly gives her a further task that has nothing to do with her normal schedule – as must also be obvious to the other participants, but they're already in end-of-meeting mode, checking their mobiles. Just before they all close their laptops, Mila makes her move: 'I don't think that's really my department.'

The social media guy is perplexed: 'What's that?' And the others have turned back to their screens. Silence.

'It's not my field of competence,' Mila says, with a slight shrug that makes her look beautifully surprised that this was sprung on her.

Now everyone is definitely paying attention.

'You always did it in the past,' the man says, icily. He's clearly in shock.

Mila decides to go all-in: 'Yes, you're right. That was thoughtless of me. Unsurprisingly, I hardly had time for my own in-tray. I'd prefer to change that. Perhaps you can get Stefan to deal with it. Wasn't that the reason you hired him?'

And what could the SM guy say to that, seeing as it was explicitly mentioned in Stefan's job description? Set and match to Mila, who for the first time has adopted a self-assured manner – and got what she wanted without being bossy. All said in a friendly tone, no pig-grunts to be heard anywhere. I'm smiling as I'm writing these lines because this experience was so important for Mila.

Stefan did take on the task and Mila has more time for her actual job. She no longer walks around with an attitude that might as well be painted in glaring letters on her forehead: 'Please unload everything here!' Her friendly and competent manner is now rarely exploited – evidence that the sentence 'I don't think that's really my department' isn't just a slogan we'd come up with for her to recite. Once her mind had decided that this was logical and worthwhile it quickly spread through her being, to become a new attitude. And once this happens, a causal chain is set in motion: new attitude = new radiance = new outcome.

As in many other areas of life, establishing boundaries is more effectively achieved by changing one's attitude than by merely applying a tool. If you say the sentence in a frenzy, perhaps garnishing it with justifications such as 'but, surely you must understand', and take everything personally (which will, in turn, affect your tone), then the statement will have zero effect. If, instead, you remain clear and calm and deliver it as though you were merely ordering another cappuccino, that little sentence can have a huge effect. It's the elegant combination of courage and clarity, together with the casual delivery, that gives you the mantle of self-assurance and has a persuasive effect on others.

'I don't think that's really my department' – an important sentence, especially for people with helper's syndrome who always get things done and feel they have to save the day for others. The hurdle that stands between them and their own happiness is often their great ability to empathize. If you happen to be that kind of person, you'll know exactly what I mean. Unfortunately, this lovely quality is often bound up with a fear of leaving others in the lurch and disappointing them. 'You weren't put on this earth to prevent other people being disappointed in you,' a coach once almost screamed at me. I was overwhelmed, not quite sure how I felt about this. I timidly enquired: 'Oh . . . I wasn't?' It's not that obvious when your psychic mechanisms all seem to point to a big sign saying 'I'm responsible for everything!'

If, from now on, you feel the inclination to clearly and casually set a few boundaries here and there, pay attention to the tone you adopt. Form over substance is the motto here. If you manage to get the form right (remaining calm, matter-of-fact, and with a dash of surprise), your message (the substance) will hit home. 'I don't think that's really my department': just say it, let it sink in and wait for the response. 'Oh . . . what do you mean?' might be a standard retort, because making a clear and substantial statement as though it were the most normal thing in the world always has that spirit of self-assuredness. And often people will be a little bit shocked.

Take it in your stride, and even if you do get a perplexed reaction just stay relaxed. That won't only help you stay calm, it will calm others as well. A good way to quickly resolve an issue.

WHAT THIS SENTENCE GIVES YOU
CLARITY
RESPECT
SAVES YOU TIME

Shooting films in New York – a dream of mine. And a dream come true when I finally take off for the Big Apple. My radio station, where I host the morning show, has granted me a summer sabbatical so I can take a course at the New York Film Academy. For a while I stay with Fay, a highly energetic woman with dense pitch-black curls and a penchant for Converse and destroyed denim dungarees. She's also permanently attached, by a straw dangling from the side of her mouth, to a large paper cup of decaf iced coffee. She mentions an address: 2000 Broadway. TWO THOUSAND?! Are there even streets in Europe that have that many numbers? Anyway, as a twenty-something sitting in the back of a yellow cab, I feel pretty cool bellowing that address at the driver.

One Sunday, Fay and I are heading for brunch when a movie-like scene unfolds on 72nd Street. A red Lamborghini Diablo is parked in the sun in front of our café and a dude with a New York Yankees baseball cap is circling it. He's awestruck. Suddenly, the car's scissor doors glide upwards and a grey-haired gentleman in a casual suit lobs a briefcase on to the passenger seat. 'Wow! Tell me your secret!' the baseball cap guy enthuses. 'What did you do right, man? I love your car!'

As a German I'm astonished, as my mind conjures up a parallel version of the incident set on the streets of Berlin – at Ku'damm 200, say. In this version the guy, definitely not wearing the cap, takes a key out of his pocket and inscribes his disgust on the car's extremely expensive paintwork while mumbling: 'You think you're better than us?' Envy is a fairly pronounced trait in Germany. Not surprisingly, perhaps, as admiration and praise aren't exactly defining features of the nation's cultural psyche. Fortunately, that's gradually beginning to change: extolling praise is no longer a taboo. A relief for most people, I would say, especially in the workplace, where positive feedback can be as rare as butterflies at sea. As a business coach I've often heard complaints like these: 'My boss never praises me!' or 'In our company, we rarely get positive feedback and no one is ever commended for the work they do.' I've been hearing statements like these for more than twenty years. Pretty sad. And it gets sadder still when I dig deeper: 'Who have *you* praised this week?' 'Well, I . . . let's see . . .' It's like a vicious circle. If people don't get it, they don't do it – a sobering assessment of a praise-starved country. If someone does 'step out of line', they're likely to be seen as a bit odd.

'Not to be scolded is praise enough' is a Swabian proverb, which at some point must have spread to the rest of the country. No wonder, then, that the US tendency for exuberant praise and approval evokes two diametrically opposed responses in Germany. Some find it liberating; others raise their eyebrows and murmur: 'Typical American superficiality.'

In fact, praise is wonderful. And admiring someone is even better!

I remember a workshop I once took part in, devoted to personal development and cultivating abundance. The aim during those seven weeks was to create an inner abundance in all the important areas of life. It was intense and there was a lot of homework. One task was a three-day exercise that involved expressing sincere admiration to fifty-three people, face to face. Saying it with flowers, perhaps, but definitely holding eye contact and being specific and clear. It had to be authentic, or we'd have to do it again. One woman flew all the way to San Francisco because she wanted to personally express her admiration to Isabel Allende. She succeeded, too. I myself didn't quite go to such lengths.

Nevertheless, we all had a similar experience – an astonishing one. We all found this task extremely difficult. For some, it proved to be almost impossible. It was like learning a foreign language. So, we'd stammer, feel embarrassed, stare at the floor. But that just didn't cut it. We'd be told to do the exercise all over again.

The wonderful thing is, once you break through that

anti-praise barrier, you experience moments of total happiness. If you praise others, you're also giving yourself a good feeling and you're sending yourself the message 'I can be happy for others!' Or: 'I can allow someone to be more important than me! It's your turn, I can shine again later.' Or, perhaps a little more casually: 'I'm big enough to let someone else stand in the limelight.' These are all boosts for our true selves. I purposefully say for our 'true selves', not for our egos. Because our ego is that brash part of us that is always yammering and never gets enough attention, because it feels insignificant and constantly needs feeding and always has to be right. The ego and the healthy (true) me – that's a subtle, yet crucial, distinction.

We can easily experience the difference when we listen to our feelings. When, for instance, jealousy, resentment or envy stand in our way, everything feels laborious, confining, and we might even feel a little bit grubby. We sound edgy and excitable as we're bad-mouthing others, yet everything takes too long, gets us nowhere and we might even destroy relationships – especially the relationship we have with ourselves. The ego wreaks havoc. But when our feelings prompt us to overcome this state – when reticence, coyness or fear accompany acts of meanness or stinginess – then our healthy, true self is giving us the chance to grow beyond our limitations. These feelings can prompt us to take the leap towards a better version of ourselves. Our true self rejoices, and we immediately feel this – which is why we always feel great when we overcome a hurdle.

*

So, the question is: where do you stand on this issue? Be honest with yourself. Do you feel uncomfortable when others seem to have it all, when someone appears to have a sustained run of luck? Do you compare yourself to them? Or are you happy for others and truly wish them the best?

And what about yourself? Can you accept compliments? Do you feel comfortable when praised? If so, congratulations! If not, here's your chance.

How about consciously deciding to express appreciation to someone the next time you notice something positive about them? It might be a talent, a character trait, something a person does. You could keep it to yourself and tell someone else later ... or you could open your heart, let yourself go and lavish praise on someone. Directly, face to face.

Of course, we've all raved about someone at some point, be it at a birthday party, leaving do or wedding. Some people never find the words. Not until they're commemorating someone at their funeral. Let's start sooner, rather than later. There are so many wonderful people to whom we could give our gift of appreciation. And the joy we give proliferates when we broadcast this message. Spread it around, and each time a bit more happiness enters the world.

Well? Have you thought of someone? Do you have the perfect recipient in mind? Or are you a person who always praises others anyway and you're wondering why I've devoted an entire chapter to this topic? Whatever the case, just sing your praise loud and clear in the certainty that it will ignite a flame in others and reflect back on to you like a sudden shaft of sunlight.

WHAT THIS SENTENCE GIVES YOU

JOY

THANKFULNESS

APPRECIATION

8

I COMPLETELY UNDERSTAND YOU, AND I'D LIKE SOMETHING ELSE

Strangely enough, the key word in this sentence is *and*. I could write a whole book about it. Seriously. It would be packed with stories about people who have achieved wonderful things with this word, including myself.

It's six o'clock on a hot summer evening. I'm sitting on a little platform I can access from the terrace of my rooftop apartment, looking out across the Berlin skyline. The city is bathed in orange light. A business partner of mine – let's call her Anja – steps on to the terrace and waves. We're working on a coaching concept we want to present to a company the next day and agreed to work late into the night, if necessary – however long it takes. I'm curious how it'll work out, since I usually prepare presentations on my own.

After ten minutes, her mobile rings. She apologizes and mutes it; now it just hums, vibrates and flashes. A few minutes later: the next hum-vibe attack. Anja grabs her phone, smiles at the display and puts it down again. It keeps humming for attention. She's obviously not inclined to switch it off. I make her an offer: 'Would you rather answer it?'

'No, no. I mean, I know who it is.' I keep eye contact – an invitation to expand. She does: 'It's only my boyfriend. He probably wants to know if we'll be having dinner together this evening.'

I'm surprised, because a glance at her watch will tell her that it won't be happening. Still, I don't say anything because I'm assuming the penny will drop by itself. No way. Ten minutes later the phone hums again. I up the ante: 'Would you like to turn it off?'

'No, it isn't bothering anyone.'

Wow, she's really asking for it. 'It *is* bothering someone. It's bothering me.'

'What?!' She stares at me, astonished, waiting for an explanation.

'Well,' I continue, 'we'd agreed to work this evening, as long as it takes. So I switched my phone off. I committed to this and assumed you did too.'

What follows is a long lament that her boyfriend works in film and often shoots at night or has to do reshoots; they haven't seen each other for ages and it's all a bit stressful. She finishes with '. . . you understand?'

I nod my head and say: 'Of course I understand.' Anja gives a little sigh of relief and I add: 'I completely understand, *and* it bothers me.'

Silence. She looks at me in disbelief. I decide to endure the challenge – a kind of Western-movie duel situation where the antagonists stare at each other. She cautiously reaches for her phone, switches it off without saying a word. Wow. And then we start working.

*

So, what happened? The way I see it is that resolution was enabled through the use of the one word that plays the lead role in this chapter: *and*. This fabulous linking word is so powerful it enables you to end a discussion in a casual, self-possessed and conciliatory way. It allows the statements it joins to be equal. That is, it doesn't devalue what someone is saying. Rather, it acknowledges it and expresses a standpoint: 'I completely understand you, *and* I don't like what you're saying.' That's legitimate. Very much so, in fact.

Still, many empathic people find the idea difficult: 'How can having sympathy for someone not involve an obligation?'

Easily. We can be wonderfully empathic and still have a choice in how we want to react in a situation. Something like: 'I understand your argument, *and* I've decided against it.' That works. Or: 'I completely understand you, and I'd like something else.' We don't have to approve of something just because we understand it. Just as we don't approve of a serial killer just because we can emotionally comprehend that the person had a terrible childhood.

Let's embrace the freedom to understand something and not necessarily have to like it.

This never occurs to some people. You can easily check if it applies to you. An indicator is whether you've fallen into the rhetorical habit of using the word *but* – the always slightly hyper and drama-inclined cousin of *and*. If I'd used it in my exchange with Anja, the outcome would almost certainly have been different.

Flashback: 'I completely understand, *but* it bothers me.' She probably would have responded with a justification, because *but* is an invitation to say *because*: 'BUT I just explained, it's only BECAUSE . . .' Whereupon I might have said: 'Yes, BUT you MUST SURELY understand that BECAUSE . . .' Reasons, accusations, regrets, interpretations, a guilty conscience and lots of capital letters. The dynamics a *but* can set in motion are quite amazing. It acts like a magnet for other vague or confrontational expressions which suck us into a tumult of attacks, justifications and disappointments. *But* never allows things to be equal; it demolishes everything that went before it. In this example that was 'I completely understand'. My advice is to replace a *but* with an *and* as often as possible.

In a nutshell, *and* is the better choice for three reasons. First, if you link a positive and a negative message with an *and*, the other person will reflect on both messages. Second, your understanding or empathy doesn't force you to abandon your own standpoint. You can quite plausibly understand someone's situation without having to tolerate their behaviour. Plainly stated: understanding doesn't commit you to anything. And third, *and* will definitely prevent discussions from turning into drama. That's why this word is particularly valuable to parents or others in positions of authority: 'I completely understand you, and I'd like us to do it my way.' *And* is the end. In most cases, anyway.

WHAT THIS SENTENCE GIVES YOU
CLARITY
SELF-ASSUREDNESS
SAVES YOU TIME

9

I THINK I'D BETTER FORGIVE MYSELF

hat's our biggest fear? I don't mean things like wars, or spiders, or escalaphobia (that's right, a fear of escalators). I mean an underlying, inner fear that more or less everyone has. When I ask that question in my seminars a frequent answer is: 'The fear of death, or dying.' Would that it were so: for if death was so fearsome, wouldn't we enjoy our lives more?

According to psychologists, the fear of dying is not generally a dominant concern. The two topics that are frontrunners in the fear race concern interpersonal relationships: fear of failure and the fear of not being loved. When I first heard this, the theatre coach in me had a little eureka moment: hardly surprising that many people nearly have a breakdown when asked to speak in front of an audience. Their heart rate shoots up, they consider cancelling, their voice fails and they can't sleep. If our dominant fears are failure and rejection, it's only logical our bodies invent a state we call stage fright. Because on stage, we experience both fears combined.

This would also explain why even people who feel supremely confident hear that little inner voice whispering: 'Time's up, you're a fake and everyone can see it!' When I do pitch trainings for companies – where millions are at stake – it always happens that seasoned managers become jittery, suddenly talk in a stilted, artificial way, develop blotches on their skin, or simply can't be the way they normally are. They are literally beside themselves.

So, I was all the more amazed by an encounter I once had with an experienced therapist in Berlin. It must have been around 2007. Back then, I'd started a course in energy psychology and I'd missed a few hours. To catch up, I took some one-on-one lessons at her practice. This woman must have been well over seventy, and she'd been recommended to me as an extremely competent teacher of the method. Sounded promising.

Since it made sense to learn her technique with a specific problem in mind, she asked me if there was a fear I'd like to be rid of. 'Injections!' I exclaimed, without hesitation. 'Perfect!' she replied, because with the Energy Diagnostic and Treatment Method (see page 279), we're glad when a client has an intense, clearly defined theme. The clearer the fear, the greater the likelihood of a quick resolution. All set: task definition, muscle test, practise procedure, take notes, check results. At the end of it, she triumphantly announced: 'You see, and if you do it just that way, your fear of elevators will have gone!' Come again? I was confused. Where did the elevators come from?

When she realized she'd just spent ninety minutes on a non-existent issue she looked startled, leaned her head to one side, paused a moment, then smiled and said: 'Good gracious! I think I'd better forgive myself.' No sooner said than done: she put away her coaching materials and then presented me with the bill. End of story, as far as she was concerned.

I found this doubly interesting (if that's the word) and immediately launched into a discussion in my own mind. Talk about taking liberties! Simply extracting herself from the situation by forgiving herself? Case closed, and a clear conscience? Yet, on the other hand: intriguing, how unequivocally and impartially she can just lovingly accept what is. Others spend years going to monasteries to get there. Quite an achievement.

So, I decided to be thrilled rather than outraged. I was just so impressed by the swiftness of her reaction. I only knew this kind of authentic inner freedom from reading books about it. To be clear, the incident didn't have a trace of amateurism. And it's not that she didn't care about me. Throughout our session she had been completely submersed in her profession and happened to totally fail on this one point. Instead of being ashamed and spluttering her excuses, she had decided to deal with the issue in a self-possessed manner and be professional on a human level as well.

No prizes for guessing which sentence I chose to add to my inner archive. Try it out yourself.

Around the same time I was also taking another training course on Tuesday evenings and I talked about what had happened in the very next workshop. There was a lot of laughter, and the sentence soon became our mantra for that course. Every time one of us got completely muddled in some task, and after digesting the initial shock, we'd smile and casually say: 'I think I'd better forgive myself.' A very relaxed way to treat oneself. Particularly recommended for professionals who consider themselves to be perfectionists. We're often very hard on ourselves, with all the feelings of embarrassment that entails. If, instead, we grant ourselves a measure of tolerance, we move from being the victims of circumstances to being designers of opportunities. It gives us the freedom to feel good, no matter if something succeeds or happens to go wrong.

'I think I'd better forgive myself.' So simple. So difficult. And definitely recommended.

WHAT THIS SENTENCE GIVES YOU
LOVE FOR YOURSELF
CALMNESS
EMPATHY

I DON'T KNOW

Where normally there would be a sea of black-and-red Eintracht Frankfurt banners, hundreds of colourful prayer flags are fluttering in the wind. The anthems of the fans have been replaced by the sonorous wails of Tibetan horns, wafting from speakers. The Dalai Lama has come to Frankfurt and the city is donning the colours red and orange.

It's sweltering on this August weekend in 2009, as thousands are streaming into the Commerzbank Arena to hear the instructions of His Holiness and see him live. I'm sitting with two friends on the meticulously mown football field as memories come back to me of how, as a teenager, I used to warm up for athletics competitions on this very spot. That was half a lifetime ago. Now it's the lotus position, rather than a relay race.

It's question time, meaning the moderator draws out of a drum little sheets of paper with questions from the audience and the Dalai Lama answers them. He is sitting on his impressive-looking throne, wearing a burgundy-red peaked cap, smiling and occasionally taking a sip from his cup of tea. The question the moderator reads out now sounds markedly bookish, with lots of typically German clauses and sub-clauses. The point seems to be something to do with anti-authoritarian education. I'd probably need a postgraduate degree in a specialist subject just to understand the question. I am keen to hear the answer, though. And I'm not the only one, it seems. Thousands of people are poised with pen and paper in hand to jot down the Dalai Lama's words of wisdom. All eyes are on His Holiness – or on the giant arena screen which shows him in close-up.

He gently sways from side to side as if rocking a baby to sleep, then looks up to the sky for a moment, sips his tea again, taking his time. And then, as if suddenly re-energized, he answers in that slightly singsong tone of voice: 'I don't know!'

A moment of shocked silence. The Dalai Lama chuckles. The moderator starts laughing. The stadium joyfully erupts. An incredible moment. His answer sounded innocent, happy, free, truthful, profound, cheeky – all that, in a single second. He says it again: 'I don't know!' And now he's shaking with laughter. Everyone's laughing. That was it, the whole answer.

'What liberating words,' I thought, and I instantly knew I'd always remember them. So easy and to the point: no stuttering around, no guessing, no pseudo-intelligent posturing while the brain is desperately searching for an original answer; no playing for time or pretending, no being found out. Just simply: 'I don't know.' Life can be so easy, so why do we make it so cumbersome in this regard?

If you're old enough to remember the pre-GPS/smart-phone era, the word 'cumbersome' will have a special ring. Instead of asking Siri how to get somewhere, you either had to grapple with a foldable map or ask for directions. And if you did that you could simultaneously conduct a case study in I-Don't-Know Aversion Syndrome, or IDKAS (please don't bother googling this, I just made it up). You ask a total stranger, who'll never see you again and who therefore has no reason to want you to like them, how to get somewhere. Then this happens: 'Binjai Park ... hmm ... Binjai Park ...' (looking left, looking right) 'OK...' You immediately know you've asked someone who doesn't have a clue, but won't admit it. They're probably about to send you in the wrong direction. The phrase 'I'm sorry, I don't know' is not part of everyone's linguistic repertoire.

This habit of making things unnecessarily complicated is all the more remarkable given that everybody who knows something knows there was a time before he or she knew it. So, why is it so difficult to admit? We ought to regard it as being completely normal.

'I made a mistake' is another of these can't-bring-myself-to-say-it statements. You might like to jump to sentence 26 after this chapter. It takes a deeper look at the issues involved. Because being able to admit to having made an error has similar benefits to being able to say 'I don't know.'

Fact is, trying to distract from one's ignorance is time-consuming, unhelpful and only prolongs our residing in a state we obviously feel uncomfortable with, i.e. being ignorant. Wouldn't it be much simpler to admit to it? And wouldn't it be simpler still if it didn't feel we were 'admitting' to something at all? The term itself implies that, unfortunately, we have to own up to something and we'd rather not. How about being glad not to know or understand something? Isn't that always how learning begins?

'The more you know, the more you know what you don't know' were the words we were greeted with on my first day at Berlin's Institute of Philosophy. My freshman brain took a while to digest this – I mean, if you think too much about this statement it does have the potential to drive you mad. That, at least, was my initial impression. Then I realized it could also make things much easier, and decided to go with that: 'This is what I choose to believe. This is how I want to live my life!' So much for theory. It took me decades to apply this understanding in my daily life.

How can this be? Such a long journey for a cheerful little 'I don't know'! It might have to do with the fact that I always had make-it-happen roles in my vocational life: assistant television producer, radio presenter, assistant film director, lyricist for artists, pitch trainer for priority accounts, moderator for businesses, C-level coach. When I was asked something, there were really only two possible responses: 'I know the answer' or 'I'll find out!' Anything else would have made my client or boss nervous. I was accustomed to delivering results.

This is probably true of very many people. We get caught in a kind of Deliveroo loop, prioritizing speed above all else, without really noticing. When a question pops up, there's this hectic impulse to have to have an answer. Say something clever, can't be that hard. Stand firm and deliver. In these circumstances many would rather say something than nothing at all.

And then, out of the blue, there's this evening with friends where I suddenly hear myself say it, and in a relaxed tone: 'I don't know.' Everyone looks at me, alarmed: they've never heard me say that before. 'OK, well, then . . . um . . . when *will* you know?' Pause for thought. Then: 'I don't know that either.' Everyone's flummoxed, including me. Wow, it's doable. It even has a self-possessed ring to it! How long did that take? Twenty years? And then it was easier than I thought. What a wonderfully liberating feeling, to pass on responsibility for once!

I suddenly feel I'm in the Dalai Lama groove. He also beamed at the crowd, with a kind of benevolence tinged with wisdom, followed by a look of pure joy. Looks can be an art form, and need to be practised too. Then I take a sip of my tea, look up to the sky, and – because it's so refreshing – I simply say it again: 'I don't know.'

WHAT THIS SENTENCE GIVES YOU

RELIEF

SELF-POSSESSION

ACCEPTANCE

11

I JUST REALIZED, THIS TOPIC DOESN'T REALLY INTEREST ME

'm watching my godchild Nina, who is four years old, ardently drawing pictures with her crayons. Apart from colourful trees and houses, she's also drawn two people.

'Is that you?' I ask her.

'Yeeees!' she enthuses, fervently nodding her head.

'And that there is Marie?' Marie is her sister.

She shoots me an indignant look. 'Marieee? No, that's a boy!'

'I see. And how do I know it's a boy?'

'Because,' she patiently informs me, 'I've written his name on his T-shirt.'

I'm looking at a green tangle. 'OK, and what's his name, then?'

Nina seems truly astonished by this question. 'How should I know? I can't read!'

It's wonderful, how unconstrainedly and adamantly kids express the way they see the world. Even if that sometimes comes across like this: 'My mummy has bigger breasts than you!' Ah, well . . . 'Why have you got so many pimples?' Well, I . . . 'You're fatter than Aunt Anne.' Thanks for sharing, kiddo. As grown-ups we can smile when we hear such honest, unchecked observations, and we'll happily tell others about these unflattering personal messages. Thought. Statement. There's barely space between the two when you're very young. And adults accept this easily because the innocence of it touches our hearts, and our rationality tells us it's not *against* us: there's absolutely no malice involved. It's pure observation and the urge to communicate. And we can laugh about it. But when kids get a little older, it's suddenly no laughing matter: 'It's rude to say that!' 'Don't ask so many questions!' 'What's the matter with you? You've upset the lady!' And the scolded child, who previously could do no wrong, is probably wondering: 'What's going on?'

I only know a few adults who have managed to reclaim this unbiased outlook, or were maybe even able to preserve it. An actor friend of mine is one of them. Sven never takes anything personally and never says anything intended as an attack. This makes the relationship we have extremely easy. In the middle of a conversation he'll occasionally and quite calmly remark: 'I just realized, this topic doesn't really interest me. Shall we talk about something else?' Many find such brazenness disturbing. When he first said this sentence to me, I really appreciated it (admittedly, after a slight moment of shock). Consider the alternative: do we really want to talk about my experiences with plumbers or my dietary plans when he'd rather not? If I imagine him telling his girlfriend, later, 'I had to listen to her for hours, rabbiting on about macrobiotic foods – I'm glad that's over!', I much prefer his brief and honest statement: 'I just realized, this topic doesn't really interest me. Shall we talk about something else?'

During the Covid pandemic many of us were astonished to see how people we thought we knew acted in ways we wouldn't have thought possible – probably not so much within the narrow circle of family and friends, but a little further removed. Reactions ranged from fear and total self-isolation to complete denial and conspiracy theories. During conversations about the latest government measures, if I sensed things were about to get heated (which happened twice during that period), I followed the advice usually given in order to avert religious or political disputes: exit the discussion highway, don't even bother to use the indicator. In words, that can sound like this: 'I'd rather not discuss the topic, we'll probably end up having a row' or 'Let's change the subject, it's not getting us anywhere.' Put it however you like, and take the first turn-off to Boundaryville. I especially recommend this for people who value harmony.

Nadine is just such a person. When I asked her if she could imagine responding in this way, she almost panicked: 'Whaaaat?! You can't say that to someone!' The alternative didn't appeal to her either. It would mean enduring a discussion, getting annoyed, pulling herself together and experiencing an evening she didn't want to have. At the end of it, she'd probably go home fearing that everyone would be bad-mouthing everyone else. Not exactly a good result. Yet, eventually, the fear of another heated discussion proved stronger than her reluctance to say that sentence. And so she did it: 'Let's talk about something else. This isn't getting us anywhere.' Imagine standing on a five-metre diving board trying to pluck up the courage to jump, and then you actually do it . . . well, it was like that for Nadine. It had the same wondrous effect. Once she'd safely surfaced, she wanted to yell: 'Again!'

Another example: a TV presenter once told me that whenever someone seemed about to tell a joke, he felt terribly embarrassed and suffered cramp-like cringe attacks. Even the thought of someone saying 'Do you know the one about . . .' made him feel awful. The equation in his mind was 'joke triggers flight instinct'. Not exactly ideal when you're having a meal with people, not to mention when you're doing a live show on TV. So, we found a better response, an I-message to establish a boundary. The plan: start by practising in everyday life, i.e. off-air. And so, when the next situation arose, he said (slightly timidly, yet with a decent portion of assertiveness): 'Believe me, I'd be your worst audience. I never laugh when someone tells a joke. You'd just be disappointed. We'll both feel better if you give that a miss.' When he said it with a big smile, it sounded completely convincing. And after seeing that people didn't feel offended and did skip the joke, he now quite looks forward to these situations. The cringe attacks have disappeared. Even during live broadcasts. The issue itself has gone away. This is often the case when we simply and briefly state our truth, and do so with the confidence gained with practice: the matter resolves itself.

Setting a boundary. This theme crops up again and again. Boundary – not a pretty word. Sounds a bit like 'raise the drawbridge over the moat and lower the gate'. And yet, setting boundaries is an expression of pure goodness. It's not directed *against* anyone; rather, it's a path to greater clarity, *for* a better mood, and *for* a return to true form. It's a demarcation: 'This is where you end and I begin.' Some people have to hear this message because not everyone is equally empathic. After all, we do this in other areas too. People's properties don't just flow into each other; hedges, walls and fences mark boundaries, and nobody feels offended by them.

Again and again I see that a desire to maintain harmony leads people into awkward situations, and even into conflicts, because things are left unsaid. A paradox. It's precisely because people prefer peace to strife that a bold statement can often be the best way to secure lasting harmony.

'Residents only' might be a good motto in a situation where escalation seems likely. Try it out: install this as an inner warning sign. People with authentic issues are allowed to enter. All moaners, complainers and energy-vampires, please move on. Just picturing this mental signpost might remind you of the sentence: 'I just realized, this topic doesn't really interest me. Can we talk about something else?' I'm certain you can say it.

WHAT THIS SENTENCE GIVES YOU

RELIEF

RELAXATION

HARMONY

Do you know Isabel Allende's *The House of the Spirits*? I particularly love the film, with its amazing cast. In one scene Esteban (played by Jeremy Irons) shouts at his daughter's lover: 'If you meet her again, I'll kill you!' Esteban is livid. Later, his wife Clara (played by Meryl Streep) tries to comfort their distraught daughter: 'Your father isn't angry, he just has too much energy.' I find this scene intriguing given that Meryl Streep plays a clairvoyant and knows full well how violent, relentless and ill-tempered her husband can be.

What can I say? She's right. At their core, people are rarely what they appear to be on the outside. Someone who seems to be a crooked character is often just lonely, the arrogant colleague is probably unsure of himself, and the notorious grumbler may just be disappointed with his life.

How can we know? If we're prepared to consider that the behaviour we're getting is probably the best this individual is currently capable of – rather than the behaviour we think they should display – it has a calming effect.

It might seem mindboggling that our definition of a hundred per cent is light years removed from other people's version of a hundred per cent. But if we succeed in accepting this discrepancy, a lot of things instantly become easier. And if this insight then moves from our minds into our hearts, we can stop taking everything and everyone personally. What a relief!

Here's another soothing insight: when people behave badly, lose their temper, are rude or obstinate, they're probably just – literally speaking – beside themselves. They've 'lost it'. Not a nice feeling, to be honest, and reason enough to wish them a heartfelt 'speedy recovery', wouldn't you agree? I'm serious. The other day a cyclist whacked the roof of my car with the flat of his hand as he was passing. I was really shocked; he was too, I assume, because the intended BANG! was muffled by the fabric of the sliding roof. I lowered the window and hollered after him: 'Speedy recovery!' What else could I say? He obviously wasn't feeling too good.

If we can manage to see the things we dislike in others as an 'offer' rather than an attack, new possibilities are open to us. We can start being amazed and stop getting frantic. And, ideally, we might even feel empathy, as we wonder what could possibly have made someone feel the need to be so rude or aggressive. It must be exhausting for them; it feels exhausting just to watch. So, it's better not to take these things personally, and to wish the person all the best.

At this point, I'd like to put forward the optimistic notion that most people probably don't plan to attack another person. Many are just trapped in their own 'film', in which they are experiencing things that aren't apparent to others on the outside. In this state they'll often confuse perception and reality, and treat assumptions as facts. They won't ask how something was meant before attributing malicious intent. We probably all behave this way, occasionally. No need to get angry. Try to see an insult as an offer.

Someone is shouting at you. Instead of following the impulse to respond to the verbal attack, you could decide to re-designate it. Your inner monologue might sound something like: 'Ah, interesting offer. Do I want to react to it? No, not right now, too much trouble.' So, then you smile and direct this decision outwards: 'Right, then – speedy recovery!'

We don't *have* to get angry. Remember, 'Before I get angry I'd rather not care.' Or, more self-assured: 'I decide who pushes my buttons.'

These are all little reminders that we are the pilots of our own lives. Others present us with possibilities, but we are the ones who decide how we want to react to them. I call it the Daily Test – recurring opportunities for us to grow.

So, the next time someone goes ballistic, be surprised. Be astounded. And leave the bother where it belongs – with the other person. Wish them a speedy recovery. That's it.

WHAT THIS SENTENCE GIVES YOU
LIGHTNESS
SELF-DETERMINATION
PEACE

'**H**ouston, this is Berlin calling!' I joyfully say to the screen. But Stefanie, who seems to be in her home office (judging by the look of the room behind her), can't hear me yet – video calls and their hitch-prone beginnings. She's frantically pointing at her ears, then takes her earpieces out and jumps up to draw the curtains. The lighting is instantly improved, the audio now also works, and I see Steffi plonking herself on her swivel chair and heaving a sigh of frustration.

'Hey, how's your prep for the summit meeting going?' I ask her. She's been looking forward to this meeting, due to be held in Monaco, for weeks. She's set to give a presentation before the entire EMEA (Europe, Middle East, Africa) management team of her company. Today, the briefing for the summit took place.

'I've really had it!' It comes out as a snarl. 'If I didn't have this coaching with you now, I'd be on the phone to a headhunter. My boss is completely off his nut and I'm not putting up with it any more!' Her eyes are shining with rage and the ring-light reflected on her glasses adds

to this fierce look. She tells me her boss really under-
mined her at the meeting. Apparently, he's cancelled
her Monaco presentation – or at least he made no mention of it.

'Why did he do that?' I ask her.

'I haven't a clue!' she whimpers, holding back her tears.

Her story doesn't make sense to me. 'Well, what reason
did he give?'

'Reason? I didn't ask him for a bloody reason!' she scolds
me, as though the question was absurd.

I'm astonished. 'Why didn't you?'

'Well . . . because of . . . everything!' She shrugs her
shoulders in disbelief. It's the sort of look you might get if
you ordered roast suckling pig in a vegetarian restaurant.

I'm thinking 'There's another topic lurking here' and I
make a note on my neon-pink Post-it pad. 'So, you'll do it
after the conference, then?'

'No way!' she says. 'I'm not going to beg and grovel.'

That's not what I have in mind, so I ask her: 'What would
be an alternative to grovelling and begging?'

Stefanie just stares into the camera.

In these kinds of stalemate situations, I like to rewind
the event, go back to the point where the client started to
feel uncomfortable. Then we brainstorm, like scriptwrit-
ers reworking dialogue and imagining how the story
would have progressed with the new lines. I ask Steffi:
'How would a casual enquiry have been perceived? Something like: "At what point do I do my presentation? I
can't seem to find it on the agenda."'

There's a long pause before she answers, almost accus-
ingly: 'That sounds so . . . easy.'

'That's the idea,' I tell her. 'The tone of voice would be by-the-by, like asking: "Has anyone seen the laser pointer? It was here a minute ago . . ."'

Steffi gives me a smile, tinged with regret.

Inner turmoil colours our intonation, the way we come across. And because we're afraid of sounding upset, we instinctively hold back. Not a good idea, because it prevents us from clarifying matters. The solution here is to find words that counteract the internal agitation – that way, the tonality automatically adapts to sound appropriate.

While I'm increasingly convinced that the missing slot in the run-down was simply an error, Steffi insists that it can't all be down to a misunderstanding. She says her boss kept squinting and avoided looking at her directly – a sure sign that he was feeling guilty. Still, she commits to talking to him as soon as possible. Clarity is of the essence now.

The very next day I receive a voice message from Stefanie. Her boss was totally perplexed, she says. He hadn't even realized he'd overlooked her. Shortly before the meeting he'd been to see an ophthalmologist and received some kind of treatment for his eyes. That's why he was squinting; he could barely see, and hadn't prepared the slides himself. 'Why didn't you bring it up sooner?' he exclaimed, somewhat surprised by this late reaction.

Anyway, the Monaco summit goes ahead as originally planned, with Steffi's presentation. And her initial frustration has given us another valuable coaching insight.

I like this story because it so neatly demonstrates how we're often inclined to take things personally, and how we create 'facts' that may have very little to do with reality. Radical constructivism – brings to mind Paul Watzlawick, who did a lot of research into this field. His book *The Situation Is Hopeless, But Not Serious: The Pursuit of Unhappiness* was a bestseller back in the 1980s. Are you familiar with the story about the hammer? A man wants to hang up a picture and because he doesn't own a hammer he decides to go and ask a neighbour if he can borrow his. Before going to his house, he gets himself entangled in a wild fantasy about his neighbour. What does the man think of him? What reasons might he have not to lend him his hammer? Come to think of it, he had given him a funny look just the other day . . . In the end, the man goes and raps on his neighbour's door, and when the man opens he screams: 'You can keep your hammer, you bastard!' That's constructivism.

There are many simple phrases that can bring us clarity when our mind suddenly decides to go on a rampage. For instance: 'I'm not sure what this means', 'I'm not sure what you mean by that' or 'I'm not clear what this means for me, specifically'. These helpful sentences are usually rewarded with clear responses. Everyone knows that this commonsense approach makes . . . well, sense. But so few people apply it. Perhaps because we feel responsible for so many things, especially in the workplace; we're even responsible for understanding other people's actions or statements correctly. It's often the case that when people aren't sure what someone is saying, they have this bizarre habit of interpreting what they might mean. We'd rather indulge in wild speculation than simply ask for clarification. Yet, doing so would make many things much easier because, unfortunately, the accuracy score of our interpretations tends to be low (Steffi's misinterpretation being a case in point). Because we rarely notice that what we think of as *truths* are really just *assumptions*, we inevitably get ourselves into conflicts. 'Whaaat?! But that's *exactly* what you said!' we bluster with total conviction. 'I *never* said it like that. Why don't you ever listen properly?' comes the retort. A totally unnecessary ride through the bumpy Valley of Misunderstandings – and very easily avoidable. *If*, that is, we decide simply to abandon the habit of interpretation and rigorously refuse to resort to it as a means of communication. That would be a wonderful decision, and we would instantly be blessed with fewer misunderstandings, less agitation and a lot more clarity.

'Do you want to be part of the problem, or a part of the solution?' the saying goes. Honestly, who's going to answer 'I definitely want to be part of the problem – that sort of appeals to me'? It seems logical to want to break with habits that complicate things. Yet, as always, if we want to stop doing something, we need to be aware that we're doing it. In other words, we require more mindfulness, more awareness of what's going on around us. Above all, it would help us to be more willing to admit that we don't understand something.

Remember the Dalai Lama and his 'I don't know' response which enthralled a whole stadium? Being able to admit something is a gesture of generosity towards ourselves. I described what I called the Deliveroo loop under sentence 10: the notion that we always have to deliver everything as quickly as possible, rather than briefly checking to see if we've got the order right.

The sentence 'I'm not sure what this means, but my presentation is no longer mentioned on the schedule' would have made things much easier for Steffi. So much superfluous adrenalin and cortisol – a cocktail of stress hormones when, otherwise, we pay so much heed to living healthily. We reduce our intake of white flour, preservatives and sugar; we make sure we buy free-range eggs and use cold-pressed oils; yet we permit the biochemicals factory in our own body to endlessly churn out unhealthy substances. Let's invite ourselves to a detox. Nip misunderstandings in the bud. 'I'm not sure what this means' is a very useful sentence to include in our arsenal of possibilities.

WHAT THIS SENTENCE GIVES YOU
CLARITY
SELF-AWARENESS
MINDFULNESS

14

I'D RATHER BE WITH MYSELF RIGHT NOW

Since my last visit to the nail salon, I know everything about Hashimoto's thyroiditis. I really do. Everything. I'm practically an endocrinologist and could easily converse with fellow specialists doing their rounds in a hospital ward. Which is to say, it's astounding how some people have this craving to communicate whatever happens to be on their mind. In this particular case it's the lady in the nail salon – which looked so inviting from the outside. She's probably a nice person, but the non-stop monologue about her auto-immune condition makes it impossible for me to enjoy her company. With every filed and polished fingernail another story crosses the narrow table. I hear about diagnostic errors, changes of doctor, side-effects. All to do with Hashimoto. She talks, I listen.

'Why?' asked Anna, a friend of mine, when I told her about a similarly bizarre experience in a different nail salon. 'Why do you put up with it?' She also asked when I planned on wiping the words TALK TO ME! from my forehead. It hurt a bit, to be honest – always a reliable sign that the feedback you're getting contains a valid point. Where there's resistance there's often also truth.

You know those situations, when strangers insist on prattling on just as you're looking forward to some peace and quiet? It can happen anywhere: during a massage, on a plane, in a taxi, at the hairdresser's. Anywhere where space is limited and there's no one else around. Is it because some of us find silence hard to bear? I, for one, love peace and quiet. To be fair, for a long time this was impossible for others to know, because I was obviously sending out silent invitations to swamp me with chatter. And this was true until I had a particularly unsettling experience.

'If you want to know the part you played in a situation, look at the result,' my first spiritual coach was fond of saying. 'You always reap what you sow.' If I apply this wisdom to the many situations where strangers poured out their hearts to me, it's clear that I didn't yet know how to set boundaries in a charming, determined yet relaxed manner. It took a tennis elbow and a visit to a physiotherapy practice near Rathaus Schöneberg – where Kennedy spoke the legendary words 'Ich bin ein Berliner!' – for me to learn how to do this.

It was the first time I'd had tennis elbow and it was really painful. The sympathetic physiotherapist spent ten minutes massaging my arm, checking for tenseness along the tendon tissue. Now the treatment proper could begin – and with it, something else entirely. As I soon realized, those ten minutes inspecting my physiology were enough for her to feel there was a strong bond between us. With a remarkable lack of inhibition, she started sharing the most intimate details of her dating experiences with me. While kneading my elbow and bending my wrist into positions I would have hitherto thought impossible, she told me in great detail about the previous night she'd spent with a muscle-packed beau from Western Pomerania. I was feverishly trying to figure out how best to respond when she tightened the verbal thumbscrew another notch: 'Seriously now, what would you write back to someone who sent you a photograph like this?' The next thing I knew, she'd planted her mobile in front of my face. Luckily I couldn't see a great deal because I wasn't wearing my reading glasses. I was in a state of shock the whole time I was being treated – not so much because of her behaviour as mine: why do I allow this to happen? Why don't I just tell her that it's none of my business, and I don't want it to be? That I'm only there to get healthy, that I'd appreciate some quiet? And could she please – no offence – just shut up?

What was missing was simply the right magic formula, the right sentence. All the things I could think of expressed the truth, but they were also too harsh. Too crude for this small room where I would continue to lie, half naked and feeling vulnerable, for quite a bit longer. 'Would you be quiet, please?', or words to that effect, certainly wouldn't have been appreciated in this situation. But when we're furious inside, we rarely come up with elegantly confident one-liners.

This is all in the past now, because I did eventually experience that eureka moment, and from that time on everything was easy. Now, even if I'm in the middle of a conversation and suddenly realize I'd rather not continue, a succinct I-message is enough to sort things out: 'That's interesting, thanks. Now I think I'd like to just switch off for a while.' Or, closer to the chapter heading: 'Do you know what, I think I'd rather be with myself right now.' This always works. And when I'm having a Thai massage, I've long since adopted the strategy of bidding 'Good night' at the beginning of the session. The masseuse then usually giggles and answers: 'Sleep tight!' And I'm free to relax and enjoy the wonderful fragrances of the aromatic massage oils.

Many people, especially women, do what I used to do. They're much too hesitant for far too long. They are afraid to be seen as hurtful or rude. So they silently suffer while presenting their perfect smiles to the world around them. This inevitably sends the wrong message: here's someone who's longing to have a conversation!

A client of mine once told me how happy he'd been when, after a long and tiring day at a conference, he'd managed to book the final slot in his hotel's spa. But instead of being able to relax, he was given a back massage that felt more like a rollercoaster ride. Even at this late hour, the masseur apparently felt an overwhelming urge to communicate. He also had the habit of interrupting his movements every time he pondered something. It must have gone roughly like this: 'And then he said . . . was it Tuesday or Thursday?' – pause – 'I think it was Tuesday' – massage – 'Anyway, he said he'd rather go to Sicily' – pause – 'or was it Sardinia? Anyway, Italy' – massage – 'The point is . . .' And so it went on. The client told me he'd started to feel giddy. He was a very friendly person, but also someone experiencing a great deal of stress and in need of relaxation. But his desire for harmony was stronger. His inner voice insisted: 'You can only relax if you don't say what you want, don't make a fuss, be patient, grin and bear it.' Not true, of course. But, as I've said in a previous chapter: feelings don't lie. And if the only comment we can think of is the one we definitely don't want to make because we're afraid of saying something offensive, we end up saying nothing.

Often, the only thing we require in these situations is an alternative sentence, such as: 'I'm sorry, but I'm not at all in the mood for talking. I think I'd just prefer to switch off.' That's a great deal better than the frustrating grin-and-bear-it approach. Or you could say: 'I just realized, I'm not feeling particularly receptive at the moment. I think I just need to relax for a bit.' The clause 'I just realized' is always excellent. It acts as a softener, mellows the impact of our statement, has an off-the-cuff, spontaneous quality. And, like so many sentences in this book, it conveys an I-message – the surest way to create daily moments of relief and joyfulness.

Frequent flyers also tend to use taxis a lot. That's been the case with me for many years. Travelling like this involves being in a constant state of dependency, and this used to wear me down. Someone is constantly telling you what to do and when to do it. There's no such thing as your own rhythm, or stride – it gets drowned out by all the service announcements: where to stow hand luggage, when to retrieve it again, when to lower your armrest and when to put your tray table in the upright position; drink up now, return your cup; strangers' rubber-gloved hands feel along your waistband, anyone can goggle through your transparent cosmetics bag, everything is scanned, including you; laptops on, cell phones off.

This fast-paced regime which demands your compliance has always kindled in me the urge to break free. So, whenever possible, I try to reassert my autonomy, reinstate my own rules. In taxis, for instance – another limited-space scenario. How do you tell a driver that there's an overwhelming smell of garlic? That the music blaring out of the rear speakers is hammering in your head and the ad breaks are at least as bad? How about: 'Is it OK if I lower the window? I didn't get enough fresh air today.' Or: 'I'm sorry, but I'm having trouble concentrating. Would you mind turning the radio down, just a tick?' That works a treat. Most drivers will then even turn it off. And if the person sitting across from you on the train is dying to inaugurate you into his or her private life, while all you want to do is switch off? 'Sorry, I'd rather be with myself right now' usually works wonders. Or: 'I'm sorry, I'm not really receptive at the moment. I have an urgent matter I really want to think about.' 'Oh, right, sure!' is usually the response in these situations and no one feels insulted. These are all little I-messages. They don't hurt anyone. And you get your well-deserved peace and quiet.

Congratulations if you don't need this chapter. That means you're exceptional. Because the majority of people do often feel torn between aggression and desperation in their daily encounters with others. So, for all those who have found this chapter inspiring: I wish you joy and success with sentences like 'I'd rather be with myself right now'. How wonderful, if these little tips make your life easier from now on.

WHAT THIS SENTENCE GIVES YOU

PEACE
SELF-DETERMINATION
RELAXATION

15

WHEN YOU POINT A FINGER AT SOMEONE, YOU'RE POINTING THREE AT YOURSELF

It's a mystery to me how anyone can find a parking space in the Berlin district of Charlottenburg without getting a ticket. Admittedly, driving a Smart, as I do, helps. But you'd still be wise to include the fines when calculating your car's fixed running costs. Long story short, sometimes I don't even try to find a legal space and briefly park safely but outside the rules – so I can quickly collect something from the chemist, for instance. That's what I did one Saturday in May. As I'm getting out of my car, a man from across the road shouts: 'Are you blind? You're not allowed to park there!' He seems extraordinarily upset and his face has gone red. I glance at the no-parking sign and think to myself: 'I can park here, though it might cost me thirty-five euros.' But it might be a bit risky actually to say this to the man, as he already seems close to suffering a heart attack – even if, logically speaking, the statement would be correct. So I ask myself instead: 'Do you want to be right, or do you want to be happy?' And I decide to say nothing.

Why am I telling you about this incident? Because when we're dealing with other people it's good to be aware of what an exchange (or an almost-exchange, in this case) is actually about. Is it really about me? This little pause for consideration is very helpful, as it enables us to retain our energy rather than squander it in a confrontation. The red-faced man, for instance, didn't have anything against me personally. If I had never been born he'd have found somebody else to shout at as a means of exercising his frustration (he certainly seemed to have issues with order, discipline and freedom).

When we get worked up about someone, when something about them bothers us, when we moan and complain, we can cut short this process by briefly considering what our feeling of irritation says about us. Is it really *this* person we're upset about, this man or that woman? Or does the cause of the discomfort lie within ourselves, and the next best person will do for us to let off steam?

'When you point a finger at someone, you're pointing three at yourself' is the title of this chapter. Actually make that gesture with your fingers to better understand what's going on. I certainly find the visual aha-effect of that very helpful, as a shortcut to identifying the source of our irritation, our anger. It usually lies within ourselves. Those fingers, pointed at ourselves, can reveal a lot more about us and are far more important than the one finger we point at others.

In one of his models from the 1970s, the communication psychologist Friedemann Schulz von Thun calls this the self-revelation level, meaning: what do the things we say and do reveal about ourselves? Generally speaking, this is a very efficient method for looking at the world. So often, we get angry at others – what they did, what they should have done, how it has affected us. Yet it never gets us any-where. The image of the pointing fingers has the power to change that.

Back to that Saturday in May. For many people, the obvious reaction would have been to accept the challenge and respond to the screaming man's opening gambit. Some-thing along the lines of: 'What's it to you?! Mind your own business! Don't you have anything better to do?' Happens a thousand times a day – a declaration of war. But there are no winners, nothing is solved. On the contrary, it just adds fuel to the fire.

A stranger will never change his opinions or attitudes to appease us, so a confrontational approach is bound to fail. It's a very human reaction, but it has rarely helped human-ity. Most of the time, it makes people feel worse.

Better to focus on ourselves and ask: 'What does what I'm saying reveal about *me*?' And: 'What does what the other person is saying reveal about *him* or *her*?' Questions that quickly point us in the direction of alternatives. Defin-itely a smarter move. Being able to distinguish these two levels gives us a clear advantage, takes us to the core of the topic of self-determination and gives us a wonderful sense of freedom.

Let's imagine the shouting Berliner had managed to get a grip on himself and realized he'd gone off the rails and was being offensive. Let's further assume he had suddenly felt the urge to reflect. Then this is how the three-fingers concept might have worked for him:

Middle finger: 'I can't stand it when people simply do what they want!'

Ring finger: 'I used to dream of becoming a policeman, but those idiots didn't want me – unbelievable!'

Pinkie: 'I don't even have the money to buy a car I could park illegally!'

I know, this last bit is over the top, but it does convey the scope of what is possible, wouldn't you agree?

Life is a monologue. That's just how it is. What we talk about says more about us than about others. That's why there's no need to comment on everything. The mistaken belief that we have to have an answer for everything is an unnecessary burden. It often results in us only coming up with the optimal retort when it's too late and we're lying in bed that night. That's when our guilty conscience creeps up on us and our mind starts racing: 'Oh, great, I should have . . .' Out of the blue, there it is, the perfect reply. Followed by a feeling of regret, because it's too late to use it.

Don't pay any heed to these belated strokes of genius and let the matter rest where it belongs: in the past. The past is the past. We can't change anyone anyway, we can only change ourselves. So, the next time you're lying awake at night fretting, or you get worked up during the day, remember the gesture and the sentence that goes with it: 'When you point your finger at someone, you're pointing three at yourself.' If you can find out what these three fingers are saying about you, you'll probably feel much better.

WHAT THIS SENTENCE GIVES YOU
SELF-KNOWLEDGE
ADVANCEMENT
FREEDOM

16

I CAN'T AFFORD NOT TO

Suddenly, out of nowhere, on a perfectly ordinary day when I'm not particularly stressed and not expecting anything unusual to happen, a little thought briefly pirouettes through my mind. It's a question, really: 'How come I'm not living in Bali?' A light-hearted yet pertinent inspiration that suddenly opens a window to the world and allows me to view all its possibilities, imbuing the moment with a quality of magic. Suddenly, the thought of living in Germany seems absurd – after all, the world's so big, and life's so short. Why not go to Bali, at least for two or three months?

And since I can't find any acute reasons not to – I won't let financial or time considerations restrict me in such moments, because they're standard rather than acute – I find myself switching into make-it-happen mode. I calmly reschedule meetings, book flights and make reservations for the first week of my trip. In this magical time that lies between the spontaneous decision and the finalization of the journey I always find Goethe's wise proverb to be true: 'As soon as the mind is directed towards a goal, many things come its way.' And it is quite amazing how many things then do coincidentally come our way. I mean it literally: they *come* to us. I go for a check-up and my dentist tells me that a colleague of his happens to be looking for someone to rent her villa on Bali, replete with luxury pool and all mod cons; a client tells me that a friend of his lives on the island and is keen to book some coaching sessions; I read about a fabulous workshop I always missed when it was being held in Europe, but now, for the first time, the event is being held in Bali, during the time I'll be there; a film team contacts me to ask if they could use my loft as a film location – the dates fit perfectly, and I'll have an additional income with which to cover my fixed costs.

Things *fall into place* when the intention is clear. Things *take shape* – another saying which hails from a spirit of basic trust in everything turning out for the best. When we're clear about our motivations, reasons and goals, we effortlessly propel ourselves into that legendary 'flow' which people are so grateful to experience from time to time. We simply take the first steps, and then let ourselves be surprised by all the good things that emerge. Suddenly, everything fits. I've experienced this on many occasions during my life.

So, I travelled to Bali for three months – a wonderful, insightful time. I particularly remember an evening I spent in a wonderful ecological resort. The houses hovered just above the sea, on stilts. The floors were made of thick glass, so you could always watch the fish swimming below, with underwater illumination at night. A magical place with a landward view of rice terraces and, nearer by, a little freshwater lake. Next to it, a huge tropical tree with lianas you could use, Tarzan-style, to swing out and let yourself plunge into the lake – paradise's answer to chlorinated swimming pools with diving boards. And it was in this wonderful place that this chapter's sentence played an important role one endless evening.

After a concert, for which I had to travel to the other end of the island, I get into a conversation with two Belgian guys who own several companies and, as it turns out, have rented a Private Balinese Villa in the same resort I'm staying in. A gigantic place, with every luxury you can imagine, replete with a butler and its own swimming pool. A world of its own. They're astonished to hear I'll be staying in Bali for another two months: 'Wow! Well, if you can afford it!'

I've heard this phrase so many times, amazingly enough from people who could afford much more than me. These Belgians, for instance. They were paying £1,700 per night. So, in the space of two weeks they were certainly spending more than I would in three months. Plus, they had a steady income while they were doing so. They could most definitely afford what I was paying. But that's how it is with that phrase: it always comes from people who have all the possibilities in the world but, for some reason, can't see them. Perhaps it's because they're so used to feeling the pressure to succeed and expand their businesses, always setting themselves sky-high targets – so invested in the future they're not able to see what's around them; so focused on what will *be* that they cannot see what *is*.

'If you can afford it!' I've often heard this from top managers who earn many times what I do, and whose companies even allow them to take a sabbatical. They can simply apply for it, and when they return they just slip back into their permanent jobs. People who own houses, sailing boats, haciendas, and get fat bonuses. 'If you can afford it!' Seriously?

Back to Bali. I waited a moment before I replied: 'Let me put it this way: I can't afford *not* to.' An awkward silence. Did that sound patronizing? And what if it did? I suddenly felt I'd had enough of people who didn't live their lives most of the time; people who crammed their ultra-intensive wellness regime into a two-week island escape, and put any real dreams they might have on hold till Day X – a day which might never come, because a stroke, cirrhosis, burnout or a heart attack arrives before it.

Perhaps I was in an irritable mood because I had just finished reading Bronnie Ware's bestseller *The Top Five Regrets of the Dying*. The meaning of life was very much a topic on my mind. Ware approaches the subject from the tail-end, so to speak. As a palliative care worker, she nursed many people who were terminally ill, listened to their stories, asked questions and eventually began to make notes. Her conclusion was that whether someone is rich or poor, at this point in their lives their thoughts revolve around the same topic: a life not fully realized. 'I wish I'd had the courage to live a life true to myself' was the top regret. That's pretty devastating. Number two: 'I wish I hadn't worked so hard', followed by 'I wish I'd had the courage to express my feelings' and 'I wish I'd stayed in touch with my friends'. And number five: 'I wish I'd let myself be happier'.

What a sad résumé. And the two Belgians I met in Bali agreed with me. After I told them about the book, we had a long, open-hearted and extremely enlightening discussion. I think all three of us learnt something that evening, and Bronnie Ware probably sold a few more copies of her book. And since the day I read it, that number one regret has made a deep impression: 'I wish I'd had the courage to live a life true to myself'. What a thing to have to admit to yourself at the end of your life. Then, even a casually muttered 'I think I'd better forgive myself' won't help any more.

Therefore, in anticipation of our time coming and our wishing to be able to look back with a sense of satisfaction, perhaps the phrase 'I can't afford not to' is a healthy impulse for the present. A little monologue that opens up new possibilities for us. As a coach, I've often seen how utterly convinced one can be that a mere thought is true. All those reasons, supposedly, why we can't do this or that. But when we do let go, even if it's just on a whim, miraculous things happen. And all of a sudden, so many things that are impossible are possible after all.

I think it does us good to challenge our convictions occasionally, no matter how true we think they are. This has the magical effect of setting things in motion. Even if we only tinker with a tiny part of ourselves, our whole system starts to shift. A wonderful way to start becoming the person we truly are.

WHAT THIS SENTENCE GIVES YOU

AUTHENTICITY
DEVOTION
FULFILMENT

17

**I THINK THIS ISSUE
IS YOURS**

Sometimes, love is simply gone, a relationship or marriage has run its course. And even a desire to rejuvenate it no longer seems realistic. People develop and move on. Or, unfortunately, they don't. There are many reasons why that passionate exclamation mark behind the words 'I love you!' can turn into a feeble question mark. And if, in the middle of this break-up, one of the partners falls in love with someone else things can get pretty nasty. If you're the one left stranded, your part in this breakdown is easily ignored and the destructive energy of loss is directed at another target entirely: the new partner.

This happened to a client of mine. She became the target of derision for the guests at a dinner party in Hamburg's très chic Elbchaussee one winter's night.

Laura's new boyfriend, Nils, is in high spirits on this evening. He's about to introduce her to many of his friends, who have only known Nils during his twelve-year marriage to Melanie. They were a fantastic couple, until they realized it had all just become a show. They went through a rough period for several years, during which they rowed, ignored each other or pretended that everything was fine. Here, on this evening, was a new Nils who was going to try to find happiness with Laura.

So, we have a somewhat naive Nils, bubbling with charm at this get-to-know dinner, not considering that the friends he shared with Melanie are now in a bit of a quandary. They would like to be happy for Nils, but they also know how his ex-wife is suffering. Tricky.

It's a lovely place, with a tastefully decorated living room leading into a winter garden. The long dining table has been opulently decked out with flowers, candles in stylish holders, and an advent wreath above the table. Lanterns in the garden illuminate the view down to the banks of the Elbe river. Nils' friend Heike is the host, and she's left nothing to chance. Everyone greets Laura with a smile and a little peck on both cheeks. It promises to be a happy event. But the buoyant mood turns sour even before the starter is served.

'So, you're the reason he left Melanie,' Heike says, rather pointedly, while sipping her punch. 'One could say, you're the reason the marriage failed.'

'Yes, don't you feel a tinge of guilt?' someone else, with an ironic smirk, hisses from across the table.

Nils is pretending not to hear these remarks.

I'm curious to know how the story ends. 'How did you react?' I ask Laura when she tells me about her experience a few days later during a coaching session on the phone.

'It was easier than I thought,' she answers. 'I simply said: "I think the two of them managed to ruin their marriage on their own – they didn't need my help."' No nasty undertone, nothing offensive, just calm and clear as a bell: this is me, and that's you. And this, by the way, is as true as it gets. Wow.

It's always great when someone who's been grappling with an issue for a while suddenly manages to be totally confident and self-assured, when they simply say what is. How do I stay true to myself? And how can I see the part I play in a given issue? Those topics have often cropped up in our sessions. And now this. Congratulations, Laura!

'I think this issue is yours' – a brief sentence that neatly puts the lid on complex and unwelcome topics. It can make your life easier in a flash, especially if you don't just say it, but feel it. If you're confronted with an issue which has nothing to do with you – return to sender. Being on the receiving end of other people's touchy subjects can make your life a misery. And solving other people's problems is impossible anyway. Still, it happens all the time, these little hijack attempts, where people try to drag each other into their respective dramas.

An architect told me that a colleague of hers was constantly harping on about how he was earning less than her. And it always made her angry. Until she finally put an end to it by applying what she'd learnt in her coaching sessions. 'My income seems to be a huge topic for you,' she said, when he next brought it up. 'Perhaps you'd like to have a word with yourself about that. Or discuss it with the boss? It's certainly not a topic for me. It's your issue, really.' The guy was perplexed, didn't know how to respond. She hasn't had to deal with this since.

We have a desire to position ourselves clearly and effortlessly. At the same time, we're afraid of failing at this.

We tend to forget that communication is a learning process. And because this wish to be seen as self-determined individuals isn't respected straight away, we easily get discouraged and give up. The right sentence can do wonders, but using pre-formulated sentences in everyday life doesn't exactly sound appealing. Many feel awkward doing so. 'I'm not an actor – it'll sound totally rehearsed' is an objection I often hear. I totally understand this objection, and I have a completely different view. We're actors *already*. For years we've been used to putting on an act to please people, or to be inconspicuous, or indeed to get attention. If you really want to feel self-determined, it's time to show who you really are: honest, free, open. And, ideally, equipped with sentences that really work. If this means learning these sentences by heart, to begin with, so be it. After all, many of us learnt to ride a bike by using stabilizers.

My advice: choose any sentence from this book, learn it by heart and then say it again and again until it sounds completely natural, as though you'd just thought of it. That's the best way to start. It's not about meticulously scripting every conversation beforehand. But if you want to be sure to say an effective thing at the right time, it definitely helps if you practise. 'Fake it till you make it' – an ancient proverb from the world of acting. And here's the good bit: the chances of it experiencing a positive outcome the very first time you try it are pretty high. Which means, you'll be much more relaxed when you do it again. Let's be honest, how else can it be done? Learning always involves practice.

What you nourish grows – just as true in personal

development as it is for plants. It's just a different kind of nourishment. Human beings achieve growth through attentiveness. That's the currency of wellbeing. Everything we pay attention to grows and thrives – in good and in bad ways. It's the energy with which we can nurture our thoughts and form them into powerful convictions. We can also make them wither, by taking our focus away from them. The more attention we lavish on something, the mightier it gets. Conversely, if we don't let our thoughts revolve around an idea and banish it from our conversations, it fades away. Luckily, we are free to choose which topics we devote our attention to, which ones don't belong to us (and are best returned to sender), which ones annoy us and which ones we want to happily embrace.

When we have the feeling that someone has 'got it in' for us, wants to 'lay something' on us – perhaps because they don't like us and we remind them of what they dislike about themselves – that's when the phrase 'I think this issue is yours' can do wonders. These situations offer the opportunity to shake things up, so they can settle in the right place. It also works like a litmus test: when you say it, you'll immediately know if it's true. If you still feel restless or upset, it's an indication that the topic probably does have something to do with you. If, on the other hand, these stressful feelings are absent, you'll know the sentence is true.

Being able to differentiate between topics that belong to you and those that don't can be liberating. Just as it is when you return the latter to the people responsible for them.

The same effect is achieved by the phrase's sister sentences 'I don't think that's really my department' (6) and 'That says more about you than me' (20). So, if you're in the mood for chapter-hopping, those two sentences fit perfectly with 'I think this issue is yours.'

WHAT THIS SENTENCE GIVES YOU

CLARITY
FREEDOM
A CLEAR CONSCIENCE

18

AS I SAID

Silke is a successful manager, whom most people would probably describe using terms like strong, high-powered, courageous, self-confident, emotionally intelligent. But looking at her now, sitting across from me, there's little evidence of any of that. She's exhausted and distraught, apologizes all the time and keeps dabbing at her eyes with her handkerchief.

She's telling me about the last time she went to see her mother.

'Every time I visit her, she nags me, says I'm too thin, heaps piles on my plate even when I tell her I'm not hungry. I have to force myself to eat it. Then she asks me if I want more, but she's already putting another dollop on my plate. It infuriates me!'

Understandably so. Let's unpick the knot. What's driving her to despair isn't really her interfering mother. It seems to me that the real reason lies in the fact that Silke is unable to take herself seriously enough when dealing with her mum. It's that simple, and it's that complicated. Silke, who perceives herself as a tough and highly motivated manager, suddenly drifts into a state of powerlessness in which she can no longer recognize that she has choices. What makes it even worse, she says, is the fact that she gets so upset about it.

Many of us have probably experienced this phenomenon – privately and in our jobs. The experienced personal assistant who suddenly mistypes everything when a particular person is standing behind her. A colleague who constantly interrupts us in meetings, even though we've told him a hundred times that we want to finish what we're saying – and this only happens with him. Situations in which we feel oddly defenceless in another's presence.

The way out of this quandary is easier than you might think. If, for whatever reason, we suddenly feel as if we're no longer at full strength we can ask ourselves how a grown-up would act in this situation, and then we can adopt precisely this attitude when responding to it. There are two steps involved in this response. First: say what you need to say. And, second: take yourself at your word. Act as if you have just been listening to yourself. Take yourself seriously. Because only then is it possible for others to take you seriously too.

Let's apply this to Silke's situation. Her mother asks her if she would like to eat something. Because she's not hungry, Silke declines. Her mother responds by putting food on her plate. A self-determined grown-up who takes her own words seriously might now think that her mother is behaving a bit oddly, but she certainly won't eat the food. If her mother then reproachfully exclaims 'But you're not eating!', the grown-up would probably resist the impulse to justify herself and repeat what she has already said. It's highly likely her mum understood her the first time – this isn't about a misunderstanding.

So, in my view, all Silke needs to make her life much easier from now on are three simple words: 'As I said'. Let's rehearse the scene.

Mother: 'Do you want some more? You're so skinny!'

Silke: 'No, thanks, I'm not hungry.'

Wham! Another dollop of food lands on her plate. If Silke manages to stay calm now and takes herself seriously, there will be a different ending from usual.

Let's say both of them chat for a bit longer, until her mother chides her: 'But you're not eating!'

Her daughter gives her a surprised look and casually remarks: 'Well, as I said . . .' If she then gently pushes the plate away from her, just a tad, I guarantee this topic will not pop up again in future.

Of course, few people believe me when we get to this point in a coaching session. Quite the contrary – I get a cascade of objections. 'What?! I can't do that! She'll feel insulted!' 'Wow, that's cheeky!' 'You don't know my mum!' Or, in the case of the personal assistant: 'I can't simply stop typing when he's standing behind me!' Yes, you can. If you previously asked him not to stand there, because you like to have some space behind you, you can definitely do that.

I told Silke I was convinced her mother would stop pestering her after the 'As I said' response – and that's how it happened. Her mum was just a bit irritated and asked what she should do with the food, before answering her own question by clearing the table. After that the subject never cropped up again. It was truly off the table. Clarity is a remedy for many things, and even those who habitually disregard other people's boundaries are often, paradoxically, thankful when you set them limits. I've seen that happen many times. So, don't be shy. Why not try a different reaction from the usual? Take your own words seriously.

And if 'As I said' is too bareboned for you and you'd like to jazz it up (rhetorically), be my guest. If the person you've said it to responds by asking 'Is that all you're going to say?', you might want to reply: 'But I've said everything there is to say. I'll be happy if you take it seriously.' Or, you might say: 'It is. My feeling is, I've already covered everything.' Or: 'I don't have the urge to add anything. Is something not clear?' And if you prefer a more confrontational approach: 'I don't think it will add anything if I repeat it three more times. As I said, I don't wish to eat anything.'

I understand the desire to be armed with sentences like this, cocked and ready to fire. I'm also sure you'll never need them if your intention is clear and your attitude positive.

WHAT THIS SENTENCE GIVES YOU
FREEDOM
INNER PEACE
SELF-CONFIDENCE

19

WORRYING IS POINTLESS

I find the idea of crowds of people crammed together in confined spaces in situations where I have zero control pretty unappealing. Too many unpleasant sounds, too many smells – it's just not my thing. And, as so often when I have this kind of realization, I go and put myself in precisely this situation soon after. It's simply the best and quickest way to grow beyond yourself. 'Stretch' was the word the teacher I most admired used for these little tests of courage where we really do get to stretch our comfort zones beyond the limit. My idea for the perfect stretch for this too-many-people-in-confined-spaces aversion was: go to India. Motto: why take a sip of the medicine when you can drink the whole bottle?

After a few chaotic days in Mumbai, an eventful train journey engulfed in a fog of a thousand and one odours, a colourful cremation ceremony in Varanasi and a spectacular sunrise at the Taj Mahal, I ended up in a little rickshaw headed for my final destination: an ashram with a tropical garden, sacred places of worship, an idyllic pond with water lilies, huge statues and a tiny tea shop. Originally, this place was designed to accommodate a couple of hundred people. In the week surrounding the Hindu festival of Maha Shivaratri we were about 120,000 more. Put simply, it got a little crowded. And while the space available for each person seemed to shrink every day, the size of pots and pans grew. I remember eating off one pan that was at least four metres wide. This was the only way you could cater for so many people. India and its dimensions! In the vast meditation hall I was confronted with other challenges: sitting cross-legged, knee to knee, on a hard A4-sized pillow, in temperatures of 40°C, men on the right side of the hall, women on the left, meditating, chanting, listening.

I recall a moment where I felt overwhelmed and numb at the same time, and in this state nothing really mattered any more. Do you know that feeling? Thirst, aches, hunger, heat, lack of oxygen – and why are we even here? All this was unimportant. It was a moment of extreme attentiveness: full, yet empty at the same time. And into this odd void, the mighty loudspeaker thundered its truths: 'If something happens that we don't care about, we call it a "situation",' the voice echoed through the shell-shaped hall. 'If something happens that we don't like, we call it a "problem". When something happens that we like, we call it "luck".'

I thought: what a compelling triad. Really, just a sober and precise summary of what the real problem with problems is: our appraisal of them. Sure, a glass being half full or half empty always depends on the judgement of the beholder – the old fortune-cookie wisdom – but hearing the principle articulated in this novel way seemed much more poignant. And then I found myself reasoning: 'When we think about something we like, we desire. If we think about something we fear, we worry.'

It can be very rewarding to take a closer look at words and phrases we habitually use. In English we say we're worried about something. In German it's 'sich Sorgen machen', which means to create or make worries. I find it astounding how stubbornly we tend to cling to our worries and how much energy we invest in them. A worst-case scenario always seems to hover as a possibility nearby. Like an uninvited guest, worry gatecrashes even the most joyful events, and, as a stowaway, even manages to get on board with optimists. Worry – what is it, anyway? To my way of thinking, it's a complete waste of brain capacity. We take a situation where the outcome is unknown and, just to be on the safe side, we imagine the worst. Simple example: a young woman wants to go to a rock concert. The mother thinks: 'I hope it doesn't rain.' If it does start raining, she thinks: 'I hope she's taken her raincoat.' And when that issue has passed: 'I hope she won't get ill.' And she could go on, of course. Our brain seems to like this game.

'Danger is real. Fear is a choice. Worries are pointless,' I once read somewhere. Yes, indeed. Fear, like worry, is mere invention, a construct, a projection. Both exist purely in our minds. What would it be like if we only dealt with things when they actually happen? We'd all have a lot more energy at our disposal and far fewer stress hormones in our bloodstream.

United Kingdom, May 2017, Manchester Arena. A suicide bomber blows himself up after an Ariana Grande concert, killing twenty-three people. One of several terrorist attacks around that time, and one of the most severe to hit Britain. Back then I had a client in London – let's call him Alan – who was extremely worried because a friend of his, Nigel, lived in Manchester. Alan had no idea whether Nigel liked Ariana Grande, or whether he was actually in the city that day. Still, he was completely flustered when he failed to reach him on his phone, couldn't sleep, couldn't work. 'I'm really worried, Karin!'

Of course, when someone is this emotionally fraught, it's inappropriate to ask the sort of questions you'd normally ask during a coaching session. That could come across as a lack of empathy. Yet I knew Alan as a solution-oriented, highly rational individual so I did ask him a few things, in the hope of easing him out of this paralysis.

'Alan, what good does it do you to worry this much, at this time? I mean, what's the benefit?' He gave me a slow, thoughtful and considered reply, but we were not there yet. I needed to dig deeper. 'How would Nigel want you to behave in this situation?' He had two ideas about this, both light-hearted and optimistic, so I spelled it out for him in the form of a question: 'Would it be enough for you if you were allowed to be shocked as soon as you have a reason?' He cracked a smile, nodded thoughtfully. I read this as a sign that it was OK to add a dash of humour. 'You know what, Alan? Worrying is about as helpful as applying a plaster before you've cut yourself.'

His features froze, eyes staring straight ahead, as if someone had pressed a pause button. Then a smile started to spread across his face. 'That's it!' he exclaimed, and looked relieved. 'So, worrying is suffering in advance, isn't it?' He was back to being the Alan I knew when he added: 'I would never stick a plaster anywhere before I cut myself!' And we both laughed. Long live metaphors!

As always, when it comes to wise, wonderful and practical sentences, it doesn't matter how wise, wonderful and practical they are if they don't ring true. If our mind likes them but they don't touch our hearts, they won't do anything for our development and we won't be able to change anything. A message only evolves into understanding when it reaches the level of our soul. Only then do we have the desire to implement it. If this sounds too esoteric for you, just read these lines again. As you know: where there's resistance, there's also truth.

'Worries are like spaghetti,' someone once posted, 'you always make too many.' There you go: from esotericism to pasta in one fell swoop. Whichever works for you. My advice: unless your job involves calculating insurance tariffs for which you need accurate risk assessments – i.e. worst-case scenarios – you should steer clear of worrying. It doesn't get you anywhere. If you can solve a problem, worrying is pointless. And if you can't solve it, it's pointless too. So, why worry?

WHAT THIS SENTENCE GIVES YOU

RELIEF

PEACE

TRUST

20

THAT SAYS MORE ABOUT YOU THAN ME

Jule is euphoric. She met this guy at a garden party and it immediately clicked. 'He was soooo charming! He made all these compliments and I felt he could really see who I am, y'know?' She runs her fingers through her red lion's mane, and her Snow White complexion seems even whiter than usual.

'Tell me more!' I enthuse, stirring the house lemonade with my straw and trying to get comfortable on the dayglo-green beanbag I'm sitting on. The beach café is crowded this afternoon and we managed to get the last free seats.

'So, the first thing he said was: "You're exactly my type!"' Jule swoons. 'How cool is that?'

'Because . . . ?' I hesitantly ask. I'm astonished: his opening line says more about him than about her.

'Come on,' Jule continues, no less euphorically. 'He loves long legs, light skin and red hair. That's me!'

Sure, I'm thinking, but I decide not to say anything. I can't detect a hint of a compliment in what she's told me so far – rather a monologue with the headline: 'This is what I like!' If he had said: 'Normally I'm into smaller women with black curly hair – you know, that French look? But this time everything's different: I'm totally attracted to you, and I can't take my eyes off you!' *Then* he would have been saying something about *her*. It translates into: 'I find you so stunning, my usual preferences have gone out the window.' But of course I keep this to myself as I don't wish to spoil her mood.

I've just thought: perhaps this sounds like I'm being ungenerous, nitpicking. Still, I'm going to leave it standing: the potential for conflict is huge when we can't distinguish between what people are saying about *us* and what they're telling us about *themselves*. Take a situation where people we're close to demand extraordinary things of us, so that they can feel better: 'Quit your job and move to Cologne with me', 'I want you to stop seeing that person', 'Why are you taking singing lessons? Are you planning to be a pop star?' We might be asked to quit our job, sell our motorbike, not expand our business . . . It's quite stunning how fervently some people go about trying to destroy the happiness or success of their friends, wives, husbands, children. Should you ever find yourself in this kind of a situation, see it as a wake-up call to differentiate, and understand what these attempts to derail you say about the other person.

Here's an example. A client of mine was promoted. Now she's responsible for a large division and has power of attorney. Her husband's reaction to this news: 'What? But you're not ready for this yet. How do you think you'll manage? Do you think you have the leadership qualities you'll need?' His wife – let's call her Michele – interpreted the message thus: 'So that's what he thinks of me.' What I'm getting is: 'That's what he thinks of himself.'

Just to see if I'm on the right track, I ask her: 'What position does your husband have in his company?'

Anna answers, a little pensively: 'He always wanted power of attorney, but he never got it.'

That's interesting. So, 'You're not ready for this yet' could also mean '*I'm* not ready for this yet, and I'm worried that *you're* pulling past me in your job.' Or: 'I'm disappointed that I haven't reached my goal yet.' There are many possibilities for what the real message behind a statement might be. In this instance I doubt that it has anything to do with Anna's leadership abilities.

So, if, for whatever reason, a reaction you're getting sounds suspicious and your inner Miss Marple suspects there's something else going on, follow your impulse and investigate.

'That says more about you than me' can be a valuable sentence here. 'Really? What do you think it says about me?' might be the response. So just keep going: 'I don't know, you tell me. What's this really about?' A second little nudge like that will probably set the ball rolling.

A different example. The other day a doctor told me he's looking forward to going on holiday on his own for the first time. When he told his wife about it, she immediately responded: 'Why are you shutting me out? Has it got to the stage where we don't even go on holiday together? Are you planning to leave me?' That kind of killed the looking-forward vibe. What was his wife really thinking? 'I'm afraid you'll meet someone else on holiday', perhaps, or 'It makes me feel insecure. I don't really trust you and, in a way, I don't trust myself either.' Whatever actually fuelled the reaction, an honest statement would have given them the chance to have a meaningful discussion. Every real issue is solvable; unsubstantiated accusations aren't. All they do is keep us agitated. Accusations prevent us from growing, they just keep us small.

'That says more about you than me' is much more beneficial than getting upset. What a nimble and effective sentence – for your private life, and in the workplace. It's particularly useful when jealousy and envy play a role. Many couples limit each other's freedom, don't want the other to have his or her own experiences. To my mind, this is a complete waste of time, especially since life is short and no one knows when theirs will end. It could be over today, in a month, in fifty years' time. My feeling is that life becomes easier when we act as though this is understood.

So, let's allow people to live their lives to the full – especially the people we love. Ourselves included. It makes us big-hearted, widens our horizons, and this attitude has the added advantage of drawing other generous, free and appreciative individuals into our orbit.

Being able to distinguish between one's own and other people's responsibilities is always useful. For this, once again, mindfulness is required – a quality that is almost always a prerequisite for personal growth. When we see the situation as it really is, and where the responsibility truly lies, we can then recognize if there is an intruder in our territory, and we can react promptly – possibly also with sentences 17 ('I think this issue is yours') or 6 ('I don't think that's really my department'). Congenial statements, all of which can help when a person has a problem. Not with us, not with our success, but with themselves. Life is a monologue – another sentence I absolutely believe to be true.

When this attitude underpins your actions, those classic envy issues are quickly dealt with. Because thoughts and laments such as 'Markus always does the board presentations, never me' obviously don't get us anywhere. Self-responsibility does. An improved statement might be: 'The board members don't have me on their radar. It's time I showed them what I'm capable of.' Another thing to consider, in this respect: people who get on our nerves are usually just a mirror for us; they enable us to see what we dislike about ourselves. There's no point blaming the mirror if we don't like what we see.

I think you've got my point. This chapter is an appeal, to mindfully keep things apart, to let them be where they belong. What's *my* concern and what's *yours*?

Let's not wear other people's shoes. Why would we? 'That says more about you than me' isn't just about creating space for ourselves and freeing up our energy, it also helps us to know ourselves better, and to grow in the process.

WHAT THIS SENTENCE GIVES YOU

CERTAINTY

ASSUREDNESS

CLARITY

21

LET'S AGREE TO DISAGREE

Eric is an Englishman, and that's exactly the impression he makes on me at our first meeting: good-looking, dry-humoured, a gentleman. He's first assistant director (AD) on a lavish costume drama that's about to be shot at Babelsberg studios, and I have to stop myself constantly goggling at him: Eric looks exactly like George Clooney in his Emergency Room days. The interview goes well – he actually hires me. Although I'm new to the business, he makes me third AD. A big break, as this is a huge set with hundreds of extras.

But my excitement is short-lived. I've barely signed the contract when he reveals how he really is, and the conflicts begin. Eric is hot-tempered and can be extremely condescending. Manners? Perhaps he is saving them for further down the line, at the premiere. The director is way over seventy years old and a wonderful guy, and as we're standing next to him one day George Clooney is on his best behaviour. He reverts to being the Mr Charming he was in the interview, though even then I can tell he's not amused when I offer a different opinion on a topic that has nothing whatsoever to do with the film. After a few ifs and buts, he suddenly smiles, raises an eyebrow, and in his friendliest tone hums: 'Well then, let's agree to disagree, shall we?'

I was impressed. Everything about this statement sounded convincing: its logic, its elegance, and its de-escalation potential. 'Let's agree to disagree.' What a wonderful turn of phrase to save the day. A good sentence for all those hopeless arguments, when it's become clear that there's no common ground. A kind of emergency brake. So, thank you, Eric, I've included it in my list of Fifty Sentences That Make Life Easier. The other things we experienced together truly didn't make my life easier.

De-escalation tools are always really valuable, I find. In my home country, Germany, the concept is rather underdeveloped – linguistically at least. Which may explain why this sentence isn't in common parlance. Perhaps it's a mentality thing. Generally speaking, when Germans disagree about something, a kind of persuasion instinct seems to kick in, along the lines of 'If I explain it well enough the other person is bound to see the light'. I even catch myself acting like this occasionally. Of course, collecting arguments and examples is a complete waste of time. Do we really think our 'opponent' is suddenly going to do a U-turn? 'Oh, it's like that! I'm all for universal basic income, then. I'm so glad you managed to convince me!'

It does happen, but experience tells me: very rarely. In discussions, we usually just regurgitate the opinions we've held for years, and perhaps we'll go home when it's over feeling that our views have been reinforced another notch. My favourite example of this: talk shows.

When it comes to brief encounters with strangers – people I might meet on a diving boat on holiday, say, or at a reception – I've made it a personal rule not to get involved in debates. Not in the sense of feeling resigned, or giving up – giving up isn't an option. But letting go? Yes. Letting go is an option.

Back in the days when I was a live-event moderator, there would usually be a celebratory dinner afterwards – picture round, formally set tables, decorated with flowers, each with a number in the middle. It's usual for the moderator to be seated at the host's table, where there's normally a mix of people such as board members, keynote speakers, politicians and guests of honour. Since I'm a vegetarian, these affairs were always a bit of a balancing act. I never wanted to make a big fuss about my diet, especially in a situation like this. So, over time, I developed this remark-able ability to instantly recognize the head waiter and whisper a confidential twelve-second briefing into his or her ear: 'Good evening. Karin Kuschik, table one. No meat or fish, please, dairy products are fine. Greetings to the chef, I'm sure he'll think of something delicious. And, could the waiters be discreet? I don't want it to be a topic at the table.' The reply was always: 'Certainly!' Great. That's professionalism for you.

Twenty minutes later a waiter bellows across the table: 'All right, who ordered the vegetarian, then?' Oh well, you can but try.

Nowadays I couldn't care less. Yesterday's meat eaters are today's vegans, and it wouldn't be a topic of conversa-tion anyway. But it was different back then. Incidentally, it was fascinating to observe country-specific reactions at international tables. 'Oh, vegetarian? My niece doesn't eat meat either,' says an American, always eager to establish common ground during small talk. 'Healthy decision, excellent!' says the Brit, while helping himself to another slice of roast meat. This is when the German fellow exclaims: 'But you're wearing leather shoes!' I experienced scenes like this on countless occasions. And I've covered all possible replies, from a humble 'That's true' to a more confrontational 'I simply couldn't find the right wellies to go with my evening dress.' Unfortunately, 'Let's agree to disagree' wasn't part of my vocabulary then. Even just as an inner attitude it would have been of value.

'In my view, everything's been said. I can't think of anything to add,' my friend Paul often says, ostentatiously, when he feels he's become too embroiled in a discussion. That's certainly an option. Just like 'Could we talk about something else? I rather fancy a change of subject' or 'I just realized, this topic doesn't really interest me' (as I proposed for sentence 11). In a situation like the one I've just described, however, that would be a bit too direct.

I once said: 'If everyone was to unload their problems into one big pile, many would probably be happy to get their little stacks back.' I do think that's true. That's why 'Let's agree to disagree' is so good. We all come from different places, we're all heading to different destinations, and all of us are carrying 'luggage' of different dimensions. We don't have to convince anyone – in most cases we wouldn't succeed anyway. So, let's just let go. There are exceptions, of course: the really big topics, like human dignity. Here, I very much hope that all people of good will would always stand up and be counted. But most of the other inconsequential inter-human tussles hardly seem worth the effort.

As far as the aforementioned costume drama with Eric is concerned, I left the production earlier than planned. After a couple of weeks of psychological intimidation, I realized: even if Eric is a big kahuna in the film world, I'm not going to learn anything under these conditions apart from how to survive from day to day, how to stay friendly when I feel like crying, how to hold tight when I want to let go. I didn't want to live my life that way. So, on a rainy night, when the last scene of the day was in the can and I'd shouted 'It's a wrap!', I went into his trailer, put the call sheets on his table and said: 'Thanks for everything I was able to learn from you. I've learnt enough now. Goodbye.' One last pained smile, then I turned round and left. He ran after me through the rain and more or less repeated everything he'd said to me before. When he was done, I nodded and said in a friendly voice: 'Let's agree to disagree, then, shall we?' Lesson learnt.

WHAT THIS SENTENCE GIVES YOU

DIGNITY

INSIGHT

REASSURANCE

22

'I'M NOT SURE' ALWAYS MEANS 'NO'

Sometimes we're torn between things. Our thoughts struggle between two life buoys, one labelled 'on the one hand' and one labelled 'on the other'. And each time we reach for one of them a big BUT gets in the way. We're unable to decide. Jobs, cars, moving house . . . all of them classic I'm-not-sure topics. Dana's quandary was her wedding, of all things. Not a good day for indecision, when more than a hundred guests are heading to the church, all of them with a clear expectation of what will happen – which, in turn, doesn't exactly reduce the pressure when you need to make a decision.

It's shortly before 10 a.m. in the quaint little chapel near Potsdam, in a town called Caputh – a name, incidentally, reminiscent of the German word *kaput*, meaning 'broken'. Not the best omen, it flippantly occurs to me, as my friend Ole sets the scene for this story which could easily be straight out of a movie. Ole is Dana's best man – so, close to the action, as it were. Elegantly dressed, he sits with the bride in the back of a champagne-coloured Jaguar which is about to drive up to the church. From afar, he can see Dana's father, who is nervously pacing about in front of the entrance, fidgeting with his tails. The bride, once more, is close to tears. She's just confided in Ole that she loves someone else, is nonetheless looking forward to the honeymoon, and doesn't want to spoil everything for the bridegroom. She feels guilty when she thinks of all the guests, and she also feels guilty towards her father because he was against this marriage to begin with, but he's paying for it regardless. Dana starts sobbing. 'I just don't know what to do!'

'"I'm not sure" always means "no",' Ole bluntly responds. He's a bit shocked himself by how firm this sounds, but the clock's ticking. And he's remembering the many times in the course of our friendship when I said the exact same sentence to him when the thought-carousel in his mind was spinning madly and he couldn't reach a decision.

Dana ponders this, nods, looks out of the window and nods again. Quicker and more resolutely than Ole had anticipated, she answers: 'It's true. Now I can really feel it. I *really* don't want to marry him! I just don't!' The chauffeur clears his throat and looks sheepishly into the rearview mirror. Ole is also starting to get really nervous. Then Dana wipes the tears from her eyes and proclaims: 'Right, let's do this.'

'Oh my God!' I say, holding my breath when Ole tells me this story a couple of weeks later. 'She really called it off?'

'No, no,' he says, waving his hand reassuringly. 'She married him. Not to would have been too embarrassing with all those people. But on their honeymoon, she told him she wanted to get a divorce.'

Wow! Well, I guess there are things I'll never quite understand . . .

What's actually going on when we simply don't know what to do? And what will quickly make our lives easier in this respect? The answer is: understanding that 'I'm not sure' is basically a substitute statement. The underlying message is 'I am sure, BUT——' and then it depends on the circumstances: 'but I don't trust what I think to be true / but I'm afraid to actually do it / but I'm afraid of what others may think of me / but I'm afraid of the consequences / but I'm afraid I'll get 'no' for an answer / but I'm afraid I'll get 'yes' for an answer and regret it. These are the typical thoughts a BUT thinks. It sniffs things out, follows trails, finds reasons, it throws its weight around. A BUT is a loudmouth and holds us back, a cowardly sceptic who rarely does anyone much good.

'Someone who really wants something will find a way. Someone who doesn't will find an excuse', as the saying goes. And it holds true. Where reasons and excuses dominate, a BUT is never far away. Together with its best friend BECAUSE, it prevents us from making decisions and always gets in the way of our personal development. And unlike a NEVERTHELESS, which can set things in motion and sometimes performs wonders, a BUT makes sure you stay put. It elevates doubts to a level where they have equal status on your personal positive–negative list, aligning them so closely it becomes impossible to give preference to one thing over another.

Could it be that reaching decisions can be much simpler than all those lingering doubts, pesky considerations and weighing-up of options might lead us to believe? An answer is only possible when we replace the unhelpful question 'What am I going to do?' with something like 'What would I decide if I followed my intuition?' Or: 'What would I do if I was totally determined?' Or: 'What would I do if I knew the answer?' A brilliant question, this last one. It sounds paradoxical, a bit crazy even, I know. In coaching, though, it can work wonders because it prompts you to find alternative solutions. And it induces, briefly, a state of bewilderment – a quality which often helps us reach a wise decision. In any case, all three of these hypothetical and effective questions are a whole lot better than 'What am I going to do?' To which the logical answer is, of course, 'I don't know' – which just confirms that we're stuck in a vicious circle.

'"I'm not sure" always means "no"' is the credo of this chapter. The sentence also demonstrates how powerful a claim can be. Its firmness provokes clear feelings in us, feelings that usually lead to actions that allow us to take a shortcut out of a hopeless situation. A good way to free yourself from the leaden energy that's attached to indecision.

At Dana's wedding the sentence worked immediately. Because it's so rigorous, the bride immediately knew: 'It's true, I *really* don't want to marry this man!' Of course, it could also have gone the other way. By being confronted with a clear 'no' to the marriage, she might have realized: '*Of course* I want to marry him! What am I talking about?!' So, if the sentence takes us in this direction, we've also reached a decision. It doesn't happen as frequently that way, but it can happen when we accept the statement '"I'm not sure" always means "no"' and then suddenly feel a strong resistance rise up inside us – perhaps, more accurately, a sense of outrage. Both feelings are extremely helpful, because it's this shocked whaaat?! reaction that instantly tells us two things. First: I actually *do* want it! And second: something is standing in the way. And if these two things are clear, we can take the time we need to sort out the reasons and objections. Once that's done, an 'I do' is happily said.

In my experience this little shortcut strategy is extremely valuable when it comes to making difficult decisions. However, if you wait until the next time you're in a quandary, things might get a little tight. Are you really going to remember it in that situation? My suggestion: decide here and now that in future you'll translate 'I'm not sure' as 'no'. That'll invigorate your decision-finding process. Perhaps you can start by applying this strategy to less important topics. Practice is always useful. Or, put another way, having this sentence in your repertoire *before* you decide to get married is definitely recommended.

WHAT THIS SENTENCE GIVES YOU
DECISIVENESS
PERSPECTIVE
TIME

23

I'M SORRY IF I GAVE YOU THE IMPRESSION YOU COULD TALK TO ME LIKE THAT

Ted is a seriously cool guy. In his main job he's a long-distance flight attendant, first class. In other words, he's well versed and supremely confident when it comes to international etiquette. I love listening to his chirpy first-class-singsong when he's conversing on the phone, his ability to sound amiable even when a topic is unpleasant. Even a sentence like 'I really do understand what you're saying, even when you're not shouting' can be charming coming from him. Or: 'I suspect it won't get any truer simply by repeating it.' Brilliant – straight out of a movie script.

Service professions in general are inspirational if you're looking for scenes to put into a film. 'The things I've seen . . .' my hairdresser always says. The cashier in the supermarket, the saleswoman in a lingerie boutique and, yes, flight attendants always have tales to tell. And eleven kilometres above sea level, things can get quite bizarre. Not everybody in first class just wants to relax, read a strategy document and then pull the duvet over their heads in the hope of getting some sleep. Those who do, don't need a fifth glass of champagne – there are, frankly, more enticing places to have a party. But there are those who absolutely want to get the most out of their money – though it isn't usually theirs. They're often the ones who wouldn't even pay for a business-class seat but want to live it up in first when the company is paying. They throw their weight around, demand things and complain, says Ted. They think it's a game, and the game is part of the deal. Quite possibly, he tells me, some people actually hope someone's made a mistake with their booking so that they can cause a fuss. If there's nothing wrong, they'll find something anyway. Turbulent minds attract turbulent situations.

'In first class, you're expected to anticipate a passenger's wishes just by looking into their eyes' was the final take-away at the latest refresher training Ted attended. No problem! Try it out the very next day. We aim to please.

Frankfurt, late January. Airbus A380. Destination: Singapore. Twenty-five minutes before take-off there's suddenly a commotion surrounding the passenger in 1A – let's call him Mr Schneider. His assistant had listed Desperados beer in the 'special wishes' section when she booked the flight. Now Mr Schneider wishes to drink the first bottle before take-off. But the caterer failed to deliver it – very unpleasant for Ted. In this price range, mess-ups of this kind aren't acceptable. And Mr Schneider has already repeatedly demonstrated that he doesn't think restraint or manners are important. He's in a huff as he sets up a plethora of electronic gadgets, even though he'll have to dismantle his mobile office before take-off. Pulling at cables, he rants: 'It's pathetic, I can't even get the beer I ordered!' He wants a word with the captain – now!

So, a plan B for 1A is called for. Although a glance at his watch advises against it, Ted suggests to the purser that he could sprint to the terminal to buy a six-pack.

'About bloody time,' Mr Schneider barks.

'You're welcome,' says Ted, keeping up the charm offensive and diving into the boarding bridge.

At last, in the third duty-free shop, he manages to get some Desperados, if only four bottles, and they're not cold. He runs back, as time's running out and he's worried they'll miss their departure slot.

Back on board, a little out of breath, Ted tells Mr Schneider: 'I'll be happy to serve you your requested beer after take-off. It's being cooled right now.'

Mr Schneider throws another tantrum: why is the beer not cold, and no, he certainly won't pack his gadgets away now that the printer is finally working. Then comes the 'Ready for take-off' announcement, and as Ted walks to his seat he hears Mr Schneider call after him: 'I hope you remembered the lime!'

The lime! The word makes him shudder, because there definitely aren't any limes on board. A friendly 'I'll be happy to check for you' won't help either. Half an hour later, with the plane airborne, Ted serves Mr Schneider an ice-cold Desperados with a make-do slice of lemon poking out of the bottleneck.

The man explodes. 'Don't you know the difference?! How stupid can you get?!' And it doesn't stop there; Ted is subjected to a tirade of insults.

But then, as Mr Schneider interrupts himself to catch his

breath, Ted, who is boiling inside, hears himself say, very calmly but firmly: 'I'm very sorry if I gave you the impression you could talk to me like that.'

Silence. Mr Schneider looks completely baffled, indecisive. Finally, he responds: 'Was that an attack?'

Ted answers in his usual Ted-manner: 'No, I'm just sorry if I gave you the impression you could talk to me that way. Because it's not true. I simply won't tolerate being talked to like that.' And then, following a further (albeit half-hearted) complaint from this passenger, he wraps it up by saying: 'I completely understand you *and*, unfortunately, I don't have the means to change the situation up here in the sky. I've done my very best. If you'd like to continue arguing about it, I think I'm the wrong person to talk to about it.' Having said that, he smiles, turns round and leaves.

And what do you know, nothing more was heard from the passenger in 1A. Last and final call for (or should it be from?) passenger Schneider. Hallelujah.

I have of course had time to tell this story in detail, but in the heat of battle it's difficult to tap into the finesse required to formulate sentences like that. And, after all, at some point everyone loses their temper. The best way to be prepared for those difficult situations is, as always, practice.

Churchill once said: 'I'm just preparing my impromptu remarks.' He also said it took him far longer to prepare a short speech than a long one. After years of working as a moderator I can only concur with this. If it looks easy, it's usually well rehearsed. The phrase often used for this phenomenon in the US is 'Very Fred Astaire', because Astaire used to train to the point where when he danced it looked as if he hadn't pre-pared at all. It's the same with great sentences. Of course, they sometimes come spontaneously. But quick-witted remarks are rarely quick, and they come to us more readily if we already have a formidable collection at our disposal. That's why this chapter contains several stylish examples gleaned from the wonderful world of flying. Of course, I hope you'll never be in a situation where you'll require this unique com-bination of understanding, logic and courtesy.

Ladies and gentlemen, I'd like to thank you for joining me on this short flight today and I look forward to welcom-ing you onboard again shortly in another chapter on how to make your life easier.

WHAT THIS SENTENCE GIVES YOU

RESPECT

REASSURANCE

DIGNITY

24

IT ALL SOUNDS LOGICAL, YET MY FEELINGS SUGGEST SOMETHING ELSE

Angelika Schoor is in high spirits. Her long search for the perfect marketing director is about to end. In fact, her (almost) new head of department is sitting right opposite her. He has already come across as incredibly smart and creative in his impressive, unsolicited application.

His CV could hardly be better: A-levels in Zurich, degrees in London and Barcelona, followed by Harvard Business School; first job was for a Geneva-based global company; trainee in a cool agency in Düsseldorf, with a secondment in New York; years of experience in marketing in a DAX-30 listed company. And, of course, as of July, Angelika's new head of marketing in Zurich. Perfect! She flicks through his application again. Business-fluent in German, English and French, proficient in Spanish. Hobbies: triathlon, speaker slams and (goodness!) learning Mandarin. And if the charisma radiating from his photograph comes across in the interview . . . well, who wouldn't want someone like that in a leadership position?

Just fifteen minutes later she walks into the staff room

feeling disillusioned. 'And? Happy?' her assistant joyfully asks. Seeing Angelika's expression, she hands her the coffee she just made for herself and sticks another espresso pod into the machine.

'Nope, not one bit!' Angelika answers, looking a bit shaken. 'I can't hire him.'

Her assistant is truly surprised. 'But, why on earth not?'

Angelika replies with crystal-clear unclarity: 'No idea, I just couldn't. He's not right for the job. That's just the way it is.'

Ever experienced something like that? The facts clearly point in one direction, yet you decide to do the opposite? Or, conversely, you were practically certain you'd be wasting your time with something, and then made a spur-of-the-moment gut decision which, despite good arguments against it, made you feel marvellous, and which you never regretted?

I assume you have, probably quite a few times. Mostly, such decisions turn out to be absolutely right. Intuition is incredibly accurate; this invisible little judge can usually be relied on. How often have we said, or heard others say, 'I just knew it! I wish I'd trusted my gut feeling!' Or: 'I felt queasy about it right from the start. I should have trusted my feelings!' In fact, I've never heard anyone say: 'I wish I hadn't trusted my intuition!' Interesting, don't you think?

OK, there are always exceptions – in cases of romance scamming, for instance, or other types of confidence trick. Though, even here, victims often report that there was a quiet voice that did warn them, early on; or they say that a good friend cautioned them against the person. In the case of romance scamming this isn't even surprising. As we all know, when hormones come into play a mind that is normally sharp can easily become blunted. It's only logical that an outsider would see things more dispassionately.

But what about intuition in work-related matters, or when it comes to major financial decisions? Whenever we had an uneasy feeling pertaining to decisions in these fields, it was probably right. And, at the end of the day, it's rarely another person's behaviour that surprises us, but rather the fact that we weren't listening to ourselves.

These are situations where we would probably have been better off simply saying: 'It all sounds logical, yet my feelings suggest something else.' So, why don't we say this more often? Perhaps because of the misconception that we need convincing arguments for a decision against something or someone to be valid, or professionally justified, and feelings don't deliver these arguments. Actually, the opposite is true, because here the message is: 'Forget the arguments! The only valid argument is that you don't need one.' If Angelika has tested herself against any unconscious bias at play, and still her instinct tells her it's not going to work, then 'He's not right for the job' is sufficient. We know something without knowing why. That's good for our heart, but it confuses our brain, because that would prefer to rely on logic. That's definitely true of the left side of our brain, the part that likes to see itself as being responsible for making decisions.

My credo: if you're aware of all the facts and have good reason to believe they speak for a certain decision, but something is still stopping you, you shouldn't do it – there's a catch.

There are times, though, when we're 'the catch'. That can be the case when fear prevents us from leaving our comfort zone, literally pulls us back so that we can't move forward. We feel like we're going full throttle and slamming on the brakes at the same time.

What to do if 'my feelings suggest something else' sounds too wishy-washy to apply in a professional context? After all, some people see business and feelings as mutually exclusive. If this applies to you, simply find a formulation which suits you better. Perhaps: 'It all sounds logical to me. However, my *experience* tells me a different solution would be better.' Or: 'My judgement of character advises me to do the opposite.'

Whatever way you put it, the statement can save you from a situation where you get bogged down in doubts. That can quickly happen when intuition is strong and arguments are weak. Then, our brain juggles with thoughts until we're exhausted and end up – still in doubt – making a doubtful decision.

Perhaps all this isn't new to you, but now you have a sentence that lets you communicate this knowledge in the space of a few seconds. Because knowledge isn't always power – not if you can't apply it. 'It all sounds logical, yet my feelings suggest something else' is quite simply much more confident and self-determined than a helpless 'I don't know why I don't want him.' You don't have to know. Your feeling (or your experience – see above) is simply saying something different. Full stop. And if someone does question your decision, you can always respond with the wonderfully short sentence 18: 'As I said.'

Trust your intuition. Trust your heart – it was there before you could think.

WHAT THIS SENTENCE GIVES YOU
CERTAINTY
DECISIVENESS
FIRM LEADERSHIP

A tiny, dimly lit pub in Hamburg's St Pauli district – 'dive' might be more accurate. It's early afternoon and it's humid. But you wouldn't really know, what with the green-tinged overhead lamps and the finger-thick window glazing that looks as if it's made from wine bottle bases melted together, blocking as much light as possible. Two men are glued to the bar, hoisted on tattered barstools. A woman is mechanically pressing buttons on the slot machine. It's possible that everything has been like this for decades: the furnishings, the dark-brown wall panelling, the regulars, the peroxide-blonde proprietor standing behind the bar.

I'm here in my capacity as a film-directing intern for a crime drama, together with the cameraman, the director and her assistant. With us here, the place is pretty packed. We're doing location scouting for the film, which is being shot nearby. We spot a massive jar filled with gherkins, and a sign above the bar proclaiming: *Come back again when you have less time.* The director asks the proprietor what prompted her to hang it there. The men on the barstools snort as she explains in a raspy voice that she got fed up with the usual suspects hogging the bar, nursing a beer all day. 'That's rotten for business when you only have six barstools – makes sense, yeah?' We all laugh.

I came across the phrase again years later, while talking to a client – let's call him Thomas Baumann. 'Out of pure frustration, I've been thinking about hanging a sign with those words my office door,' he tells me. We're sitting in a hotel lobby after a workshop I held for his leadership team. He sounds stressed. I'm imagining the effect it would have, someone standing outside his office confronted with the message *Come back again when you have less time*. Quite a statement. Still, a bit more humorous than *Keep it short*, I tell him, grinning. He responds with a forced smile. He seems nervous. The lobby's rust-coloured fireplace with its soothing crackle, his favourite Burgundy in hand – these things seem lost on him. Mr Baumann is unable to relax.

'It goes with the job,' he says. 'There's always so much to do. I could spend the whole day reading emails and answering questions, but I never get round to actually doing my job!' This is a frequent complaint from business executives. 'The dreadful habit of ccing everyone doesn't help,' Mr Baumann adds, and this does surprise me, because, well, he's the boss. As the owner and managing director of the company, surely it's up to him which mailing lists he appears in.

But often, intent and awareness of the circumstances aren't sufficient to change behaviour, or indeed organizational structures. Sometimes our character stands in the way. Someone like Mr Baumann – generally open to ideas and discussions, accessible and enthusiastic – isn't exactly a candidate for winning Olympic gold in the discipline of setting boundaries. Quite the contrary. People love to consult with people like Mr Baumann because they appreciate someone who listens. 'He devotes so much time to me,' his employees think. 'Everyone's stealing my time,' is what Mr Baumann thinks, as he continues his struggle to keep up with his to-do list. It's like a relay race against yourself. It's not surprising that people like that always seem hounded.

Here's a question: is it possible to lag behind time, or to catch up with it? Is it true when we say 'I don't have time for this'? Is it even possible to have too little time when we all have the same amount every day? Or is it like the Norwegian proverb 'There's no bad weather, only bad clothes' – which is to say, if you're short of time, you're using it badly?

I'm not an expert in time management; I'll leave all the clever tips and techniques to the David Allens of this world. However, there is one thing I do know. No matter how smart the time management and prioritizing strategies we adopt are, that uncomfortable moment will come when we're overstretched because someone dumps an additional project on us, slams a file on our table, raises a question which needs to be dealt with. And we realize that we don't want anything to do with it because the time left to do our own work is running out.

When that situation arises, we can forget all those clever tools for a moment and, instead, focus on finding the right words to express our position. 'Sorry. I'd like to help, but I simply can't. Unfortunately, I just don't have the time. Couldn't you ask someone else?' That's what a lot of people say in this situation. Sounds suspiciously like the language of low status, as if our hands were tied. 'Sorry . . . can't . . . unfortunately . . . don't have . . . couldn't you . . .' You might as well run around wearing a T-shirt with the slogan 'Victim of Circumstance'. There isn't a spark of creative energy in there, not a hint of self-determination – and it's unlikely to have the desired effect. In fact, a half-hearted response like this can become an invitation to another round in which you're up against the ropes. So, how to decline?

A wording that expresses self-responsibility and pur-posefulness is always a good place to start. Let's apply our tried-and-tested I-message principle, with a dash of self-determination, e.g. 'I don't want to spend time on this now. I'm fully immersed in project XYZ.' *Wanting* or *choosing*, rather than being *unable* to. An important difference.

' "I don't want to spend time on this"? You can't say that!' is the standard reaction to this suggestion. 'It sounds rude, as if I don't feel like working.' Really? I see it differently. To want or choose something sounds more like taking respon-sibility; it expresses that you have reached a decision based on a professional and honest evaluation of the circum-stances. That's always a good message to convey about yourself. It demonstrates self-leadership and acumen. And if you manage to combine clarity of message with calmness of expression, it will come across as pretty convincing.

Will everyone like it? No, definitely not. Will they accept it? Yes, most likely. Because you are displaying precisely the attitude business leaders tell me they really value: a willing-ness to take responsibility and make decisions. 'The ability to say "no" occasionally, taking a stance' is what they tell me they appreciate. Sure, it feels slightly uncomfortable for a moment, but it comes across a lot better than the hapless alternatives: 'I can't manage that as well', or 'I've got plenty to do already', or 'There's just no way I can work on that as well. Do you know how much overtime I've already accumulated?' Nobody really wants to hear stuff like that. In my opinion, not even those saying it.

'OK, but I doubt I'll have the courage to say it like that,' some interject at this point. I don't think this is about courage. No one is asking you to remove your helmet while you're floating in outer space. It's more to do with self-responsibility: can I do my work in a professional manner if I take on an additional task? Can I honour my prior commitments? Being capable of setting priorities in a realistic way has more to do with professionalism than courage. And this is true at all levels within a hierarchy – hotel director or bellboy, father or daughter. Being able to assess one's own abilities and goals and staying true to oneself is always good, in business as well as in one's private life.

And if you were wondering how the story with Mr Baumann ended: he decided to deal with his time-management issues by taking note of himself, rather than put that notice on his door. 'I don't want to spend time on this.' A victory for politeness over desperation and sarcasm.

26

I MADE A MISTAKE

I t's shocking how rarely people seem to be able to say this simple sentence: 'I made a mistake.' But after more than twenty years working as a business coach I can say that, regrettably, it isn't easy. Also, the higher a person's status in the business hierarchy, the less willing they are to concede a mistake. That's doubly unfortunate because the actions of managers affect a lot of people. It's only when you get to the very top of a company, where competition from those around you isn't as fierce and honest feedback is rare, that this little sentence which can save us so much time and frustration reappears: 'I made a mistake.' How so? Probably because inner poise and self-assurance tend to grow along with responsibility. And these are qualities we need, to be able to state clearly and unequivocally that, unfortunately, we were wrong on this or that matter. So, to err may be human, but that doesn't mean it's easy for humans to admit to it.

Heads of division conference in a Frankfurt skyscraper. Behind me, the floor-to-ceiling windows offer a view of the skyline; next to me, my client is impatiently drumming his fingers on his laptop. It's job-on-the-job day, and I'm following him as if I were his shadow. I experience everything he experiences. I don't comment, but I make notes about anything relevant for the evaluation that evening. Depending on how confident they feel, clients will explain my presence to colleagues by saying I'm a journalist, a consultant, an auditor, an author . . . or a coach. Today, I'm a coach.

Apart from us, eight colleagues of my client are sitting around an oval table. A thorny matter is being discussed, a bad decision which has cost the company 720,000 euros. The responsible head of division tries to mitigate the issue with feeble, passive sentences like 'It was something that was agreed weeks ago. There was a discussion about it and the policy was clear . . .' He would do himself and the others in the room a big favour if he simply stated what is clear to everyone, something along the lines of 'I completely misjudged it – huge mistake. Let me see what I can do to fix it.' Instead, he keeps beating about the bush, and no one is prepared to state the obvious. The discussion widens, gets louder, and everyone seems to be getting increasingly agitated, or focusing on their own issues, sending emails and typing messages into their phones.

Eventually, someone blows a fuse: 'Could we finally move on and get to *my* agenda? I've got a call with Chicago in fifteen minutes!'

Suddenly everyone's wide awake again, checking their watches, as they've got urgent calls to make too. End of story: the conference lasts forty-five minutes longer than scheduled, and half of the participants rush off before it's over and arrive late for their next meeting. At a rough guess, fifty other people in follow-on meetings have been delayed because of one division head's inability to carry the can. They all now have to adapt their agendas, having had too little or no time to discuss their points. This domino effect will continue into the evening. The issue with the 720,000 euros still hasn't been adequately dealt with and, consequently, everyone's in a bad mood.

The takeaway here is: people who don't accept responsibility for their mistakes waste other people's time and energy and lose a fair bit of the respect those other people had for them.

You don't have to be a divisional head to appreciate this story. The same thing happens a million times a day in totally different settings: the person at the information stand in the shopping mall who has already sent you on a wild goose chase twice, because he'd rather think he's right than check to see where the locksmith really is; the lady at the check-in desk who knows full well you missed your flight because she sent you running to the wrong gate, but can't manage to say: 'I'm sorry, it was my mistake.' If your hairdresser uses the wrong colour on your hair and you're carrying the result around with you, like a travelling exhibit, it would at least be decent of her not to insist that this has always been your exact shade. People's urge to make up excuses is simply far more pronounced than their desire to admit an error and make life easier for others, including themselves. It could be so simple. Sorry. I. Made. A. Mistake. Five words. Three seconds. Done.

If we knew how much vital energy this admission gives

us, knew of the lightness and scope it imparts to our hearts, we'd surely do it more often. This tiny statement also noticeably enhances our sense of competence and self-assurance. To confidently own (up to) one's own mistakes has always been a reliable way to disempower detractors. What more can happen once you've pre-empted the unpleasantness of an accusation? The golden rule when it comes to mistakes: always emphasize the negative. If you simply say what it is, it'll improve your situation promptly. It switches the focus from the problem to the solution – you automatically look for ways to move ahead. Admitting an error has a disarming and incredibly calming effect – on yourself and, of course, on all the others concerned.

'If you make a mistake, do so happily!' is an important rule of improvisation theatre. I love this attitude! But when I suggest this strategy during the warm-up phase of a business workshop, some people are outraged: 'Errors? Mistakes? I'd rather not! And, *happily*? No way!'

Unfortunately, many people translate 'mistake' as 'failure'. I try to imagine what the result would be if we had applied this aversion to mistakes when we were infants. We probably wouldn't have learnt how to speak, or to walk, and we'd still be crawling and mumbling to this day. It's all the more astounding when one considers that most great insights have been inspired by errors. Inventors know this. If you've experienced darkness a thousand times, you'll eventually know how a lightbulb needs to be designed and its wires soldered for there to be light.

A mistaken belief I encounter again and again when

I'm coaching is that there must be some mega-tool that can counter every challenge. We'd always be quick-witted and know what to say. Bang! I rather think that in our frenzied search for the ultimate rhetorical trick we overlook the obvious. Which is to say what is. That's all you need to do.

And now I'm instantly going to contradict myself by mentioning a tool – simply because labels are easy for us to remember. I call this one STOP. It stands for State The Obvious Promptly. A small tip for a big effect. 'I made a mistake' is a STOP sentence. This advice would have served our head of division extremely well. It is quite possible that the 720,000-euros debacle could have been solved.

I cordially invite you to discover the benefits of the sentence 'I made a mistake'. Use it as often as you can manage. Once it is aired, a discussion immediately takes a turn for a more constructive outcome. It's a simple sentence. It's easily said. It's good for everyone involved. It's liberating. We would all have much more fun, make bolder decisions and experience more personal growth if we incorporated it into our verbal repertoire. I would admit it if I was mistaken. But in this case I'm sure I'm right.

WHAT THIS SENTENCE GIVES YOU
TIME
RESPECT
SELF-ESTEEM

I MADE A MISTAKE

27

I'LL JUST FINISH THIS FIRST

It's a beautiful late summer day in Munich, with a picture-perfect Bavarian sky in the federal state's colours of blue and white – a sprinkling of clouds in the deep-blue firmament. Today is sales training for a team from a DAX-30 blue-chip company. Two days, seven men, one woman. The participants are all around forty years old, and most of them display that typical casually flippant salesperson demeanour: never lost for words, always pleased to have the last and always up for a quip. A lot of competitive energy is bundled in this conference room, which looks like a film set and is simply called Garage. Experience has taught me that when people with large egos and a strong urge to communicate come together, non-stop chatter is the order of the day, and tranquil and insightful moments are few and rare. It's my task to guide their impulses, so that mindfulness and empathy can establish themselves and grow within the group. Not an easy task. The only female in the team – let's call her Judith – seems to have similar thoughts. She gives me an almost pleading look from out of the swirl of oneupmanship.

However, Judith won't engage without being prompted; when I ask her something, her answers are short and timid. Twice, she allows a colleague to brusquely interrupt her – he obviously thinks what he has to say is more interesting. But gradually she starts to assert herself, culminating in the complaint: 'You keep interrupting me, I want to finish what I'm saying!' It's no use though. Once an atmosphere is charged, like it is here, I've never heard someone say: 'Oh, right, sorry, please continue what you were saying.' Quite the contrary. Now, her colleague starts referring to her in the third person and is only talking *about* her: 'She wants to finish her sentence. But, why doesn't she just do that? I'm doing it too!' Sounds like we have a mansplaining issue here. I won't countenance that for long, but for now I'm letting it pass – occasionally, such situations create a friction where people trip over their own behaviour and it becomes apparent to everyone that they're out of line.

During the break, Judith approaches me and we're able to have a few words in private, on the terrace. Now she's telling me herself how uncomfortable she feels: they never allow her to finish, and if she complains, it only makes things worse. Since we're pressed for time I give her a crash course on I-messages, ending with the tip: 'Don't say what they're *not allowing* you to do, and what the others *should do*. Just say what *you will do*. In that instant. Your new sentence is: *I'll just finish this first*. Voice firm, meet their gaze.'

Judith wrinkles her nose. 'That's supposed to work?'

'Give it a try,' I tell her, and I take a last deep breath of fresh air before jumping back into the fray. For the next few hours we'll be stuck in that room again, with windows that can't be opened. Who was the architect who came up with that bright idea?

Half an hour later, we all witness Judith's breakthrough. I can actually see her building up to it. And then: 'I'll just finish this first.' Nice and loud.

'You what?' her dumbfounded colleague responds.

'I'll just finish this first,' Judith repeats, a little firmer, raising her palm then continuing where she'd left off. And, suddenly, her adversary is silent.

A nice little I-message is always more effective than a frustrated plea. If there's one thing we've learnt from all those political talk shows, it's that 'Let me finish, will you?' very rarely works. But if you clearly and calmly state *what is* – STOP (State The Obvious Promptly) – you're far more likely to succeed. I introduced this tool under the previous sentence (26), and it will come up a few more times because, quite simply, STOP works.

I remember the time I was standing in a queue in a flower shop. It was a long queue, as if it were Mother's Day and Valentine's Day in one. I was surprised no one had made a fuss yet. Barely had I thought this when someone at the back, with inimitable Berlin brusqueness, barked: 'Can't you open a second till?' I had to smile, curious as to what the response might be. 'I wasn't expecting a coach-load of people,' the cashier hollered back in the same dialect – but quite calmly, and not hurrying up one little bit. End of discussion. The Berlin comedian Kurt Krömer, famous for his irreverent off-the-cuff attitude, couldn't have done it better.

To pass the time I took a look at some mini orchids, taking a small step to my right to give them a closer inspection.

The woman standing behind me saw this as a chance to barge past me and take my place. Takes some chutzpah, I thought, but with little inclination to react. Then, out of sheer curiosity, I changed my mind and stepped in front of her. With just a hint of a smile I said: 'I'll just return to my place, then.'

There it is again: the combination of an I-message with STOP. As expected, I only got an astonished look from her – the stereotypical reaction to statements which don't require an answer. Works every time, I thought, even as I could hear the lady grumbling to herself. What could she have said to me when there was no attack to respond to? Always good to test one's own recipes occasionally.

Life gets easier when we make a conscious decision not to reward an irritation by staging a drama. Otherwise, a minor itch can turn into a major headache. Better to withdraw your energy immediately – and, armed with the right sentence, that can be quickly done.

Most of us underestimate ourselves. 'That's more easily said than done' is a common response. 'It's only natural to get angry in a situation like that.' Hmm. Why do so many people think it's natural – human, that is – to be the victim of our feelings, when it's clear that we produce those feelings ourselves? They are a reaction to our thoughts, which we also make ourselves. Homemade, of our own free will. It *is* simple to cool down again. We just haven't practised it, or it never occurred to us; perhaps we never tried. My experience is: taking possession of your own space, standing up for yourself and being calm or self-assured *is* pretty easy once we decide to make this commitment and strike this deal with ourselves. Otherwise, it won't work – I'll gladly concede that point to all the sceptics. Getting het-up is a matter of choice, and exiting the drama is just a decision away.

The louder we shout NO – at ourselves, at the circumstances, at other people – the louder the world shouts NO back at us. That's the law of attraction, and it's been that way since long before books titled *Law of Attraction* started filling shelves in the esoteric sections of bookshops. To my mind, the phenomenon has more to do with common logic than specialized knowledge anyway. The phrase 'What goes around comes around' has been used for generations. That like attracts like is something I've experienced a thousand times – with others and with myself. So, let's be mindful of the messages we send, of our thoughts and our feelings.

Sometimes, I go on a little fantasy trip. I imagine that someone is filming our lives, every second of them. And every evening, when we sit down to view the rushes, we see the bits where we got really mad about something. We wouldn't like it. We might laugh at other people's actions, but at our own? We'd probably be embarrassed – I certainly would. The next time I was in a stressful situation I'd quickly calm down and do my best to produce a better film. One that I'd like to watch. Try it out sometime. It usually works well. And if it doesn't, sentence 9 will help: a soft, melodic rendition of 'I think I'd better forgive myself.'

Life, it seems to me, is like a big game with lots of little daily tests which help us to grow, or which we fail – exactly like the situation with Judith and the sales team in Munich.

Of course, it would be fantastic if people just let others have their say. But, if someone does interrupt you, it helps not to take it personally and to simply state what will happen next: 'I'll just finish this first.' Sounds clear, self-evident, and not as if you're bristling for a fight. The best formula to actually reach your goal. With kind regards to all those political talk shows on television.

WHAT THIS SENTENCE GIVES YOU

FREEDOM
RESPECT
DIGNITY

28

I'VE TAKEN NOTE

Sometimes life spoils us. Out of the blue you get an offer that makes you want to jump for joy. That happened to me just before the new millennium on a wet and cold November day.

'Fancy helping me film some reports in Cape Town?' Frank hollers into his mobile, trying to be heard above the roar of the wind. I'd only met him a few weeks earlier, at a press conference.

'Doing what, exactly?' I ask, a bit dumbfounded. I've never done TV reports before.

'Well, you could do interviews, so I'll get some decent soundbites, and the preps for those. You could walk through the scene when I need an extra. So, editorial stuff and feel-good management, mainly. Your English is better too. I'll do camera and editing.'

The guy's either mad or unprofessional, or he knows something I don't. Why does he think I'd be right for the job?

As if he can hear my thoughts, he continues: 'It's all been arranged with South African Airways. They're sponsoring two first-class flights.'

'OK, well . . . a really tough decision,' I tease him. 'Yes, you've convinced me!'

'That's settled, then,' he says, and a moment later he's gone, leaving me thinking: 'Isn't it summer in South Africa now?'

A week later I'm sitting with Frank and Kai on the terrace of the legendary Mount Nelson Hotel – a pink dream of a place, though the colour clashes with my sunburn. Fluttering beneath a stone on the table is our ambitious work schedule: five reports in five days, jotted down on five sheets of paper. The first one will be shot right here, which, I've just been told, is why our stay at the hotel won't cost anything. (I should definitely consider doing more travel journalism.) The second location will be Grootbos, between Van Dyks Bay and Stanford – a luxurious private nature reserve, destined to become famous twenty years later as the location for *Sing meinen Song* ('Sing My Song'), a popular reality TV show in Germany.

Both places are perfect for a travel report. But the mood is not the best. Frank is constantly berating Kai, a German friend of his living in Cape Town who organized all our shooting permits. Frank is hectic, and a bit too loud. He demands, stipulates, asks questions, but doesn't wait for a reply. 'I really want you to understand this!' he's now saying for the third time.

Suddenly Kai interrupts Frank. Clearly and calmly, he says: 'I've taken note.'

'What?!' Frank splutters, like a car skidding to a halt.

Kai says it again: 'I've taken note.'

A sentence like a stop sign. Frank is perplexed, but quickly calms down, orders a Singapore Sling. And we can all sit back and enjoy the beautiful vista of the Mount Nelson.

Surprisingly effective, this little statement, and hereby officially added to my wonderful archive of sentences. It says the same as 'I heard you' but with a little more calmness and authority, enabling you to reclaim some territory. 'I've taken note.' It has a strangely formal ring to it, sober, official-sounding. This lends gravity to the words.

I recall a recalcitrant, disruptive manager in one pitch workshop; red face, crewcut, very tight shirt over a very large belly. We've hardly got through the first ten minutes and he has almost succeeded in undermining the unity of the group. He complains, scuppers the round of introductions, types on his mobile. When he's speaking to me, he looks somewhere else; when someone else talks, he interrupts them. The guy's a human time bomb, and it's clear I'll need to intervene to get us back on track. That's the message I'm receiving from the others as well: from curious-as-to-what-will-happen right up to pleading, the looks on their faces say it all.

As I'm introducing a new concept, he starts grumbling again. I stop, and address him directly: 'Just a moment. My suggestion is that you should be getting a lot more attention. You obviously have a great deal to say.'

There it is, the first time he spontaneously looks me in the eye. 'What do you mean by attention?' he barks, and his face gets even redder.

'Well, we don't know each other yet, but it seems to me you have a lot to say. And, I'd obviously like to hear it. So, please . . . How are you feeling, incidentally?'

After a dismissive gesture, he actually starts to talk. About the pointlessness of workshops, that soft skills are strictly something for women, that he doesn't need any of that, and that he can't do his job right now because I'm stealing his time.

'That's horrible for you, then, isn't it?' I say.

'Bloody right!' Mr Crewcut snaps.

'Well,' I say, 'I suggest that you really concentrate for one hour, that you're really present, and give it a chance. And if it's just as terrible for you at eleven o'clock, you should definitely leave the room because it's just not on – it would be a complete waste of your time.'

He embarked on a little speech, and when he ran out of words, I said: 'Good. It's reached my attention. You've said everything, we've all heard it. So, shall we continue?'

From that point on it was a pleasure to be there and I could finally do my job. The man stayed till the end of the course.

'I've taken note', 'It's reached my attention', 'I've heard you clearly' – all sentences that convey the same meaning: 'Your message has been received'. That's why they work. Sometimes people just want to hear that they're being heard. Then, whatever was troubling them seems almost to vanish. Let's do them the favour. Life can be that simple. 'I've taken note' is basically a confirmation of receipt, as we're familiar with in other areas. For instance: 'We have received your email and your request is being processed' – good to know that your message will be dealt with. No one, or very few people, send messages in bottles.

Have you ever asked yourself why people shout, why someone is behaving aggressively? Perhaps out of desperation. Maybe they just don't know how else to react. Not knowing how to do something makes a person even angrier. And what lies beneath that? From a psychological perspective, the answer is simple: we shout when we feel we are not being heard. That's all. We're familiar with it from our daily lives. If your girlfriend is on the other side of the street, you have to call out to her to be heard; if she's sitting next to you in the cinema, you're not going to shout in her ear. So, if someone who's shouting thinks he's not being heard, it's clear which de-escalation strategy is likely to work. Send an acknowledgement – 'I've taken note' – and, in most cases, that will be sufficient to reassure them and calm things down.

WHAT THIS SENTENCE GIVES YOU

REASSURANCE
A CHANCE TO CHANGE THE TOPIC
SELF-DETERMINATION

29

I'VE CHANGED MY MIND

'**D**amn, I shouldn't have done it!' Til sighs. For days he's had this dull ache in his stomach and he's been wondering what brought it on. Just now, it suddenly dawned on him. 'I just don't want to work for this client!' he moans, and then with even more torment in his voice: 'Why on earth did I agree to it? Not good. NOT. GOOD. AT. ALL.' He wriggles around restlessly on his oddly shaped designer chair, then jumps up and stands by the window, staring out.

Today is our wrap session in Düsseldorf, meaning our last day of coaching. Always a good time to look back on what's been achieved. What was our goal three months ago? What were the highlights along the way, the most important insights? Has it all, in fact, been a waste of time? Because, right now, Til's issues with self-leadership – a topic we dealt with in our very first session – have returned like a boomerang that's whizzing through this long, elegantly designed conference room with its spectacular views of the river Rhine (could that possibly be Cologne over there?).

'How am I going to get out of this one?' he's mumbling, still staring into the distance. It's a question that's often asked during coaching – equally relevant in business and private affairs. Anyone who is conscientious and takes commitments seriously will naturally feel awkward when they cancel something. Our mind doesn't like it, our heart even less. It's an affront. We don't want to be like that. It's little wonder, then, that our brain frantically searches for a way out when a cancellation is looming. Unfortunately, there isn't one: a 'no' is a 'no', and that's precisely how the recipient understands it. 'There must be some kind of soft-ener,' Til pleads. 'When *you* say difficult things it always sounds easy.' That sounds more like the goal-oriented busi-ness consultant he is, head of a unit with 1,200 employees. He's used to making decisions not everyone likes. Yet, he's talking washing machines – or at least that's what the term 'softener' reminds me of. He wants something to mitigate the harshness. He's going to retract his offer, but he wants to do it with words that make the decision seem light and bouncy.

Even before I've made a suggestion he's reeling off a list of possible white lies – a tempting option, as white lies always sidle up to us when we have a guilty conscience. Soon they're barging ahead of all other ideas as they con-fidently proclaim: 'Choose me and your life will instantly be much easier!' Often enough, we actually believe what this rebellious inner voice is telling us, though it seldom speaks the truth. A guilty conscience simply isn't a good adviser, and it precludes us from acting in a composed and confident manner. But that's exactly what we need when we're in a spin and want to regain control. In these moments a clear and self-assured statement is required to reinstate us as pilot of our destiny. For example: 'Concerning the commitment I made the other day: after giving it more consideration, I realized my decision had been much too hasty. It simply doesn't fit. I've changed my mind.'

That, or something along those lines, could be a first draft, so to speak. And then, see how it goes. The other person will most likely be startled; worst case, they'll be indignant. Let's play it through. 'What? But, why? You sounded sure of yourself! You committed to it!' That would be the reproachful reply. An important tip, here: don't let this jolt you into reeling off long-worded excuses. Better to clearly and calmly restate your position: 'You're right, I did. Then I realized it was a bad idea. It just doesn't fit. I misjudged it and now I've come to a different decision.' Notice something? Lots of words, no concrete reasons given – not one. Instead, the clear and assured focus on changing your decision. A very simple message, yet most people can't see it when white lies and justifications collude to fog up our minds. Give yourself permission not to have to explain everything. 'It simply doesn't fit for me' is usually quite sufficient. 'I've reached a different decision' too. Most people react much better to this than we imagine. Once again, this is due to the powerful I-message. And 'I've changed my mind' comes across as clear, straightforward, natural and agile. Importantly, it also says: here is a person who is taking responsibility by making a clear choice.

How much worse the classic 'Something important came up' sounds in comparison, the standard excuse that is never well received because translated into clear English it obviously means 'You're not as important as the thing that came up', or to be precise, 'Other people are more important than you are.' The ego doesn't like that. And the ego is always eavesdropping when it suspects we're being slighted.

'Life got in the way,' someone once wrote to me. I could well understand that. Life has its own agenda and can ruin our long-cherished and carefully crafted plans. Or, as John Lennon put it: 'Life is what happens while you're busy making other plans.'

We don't need to succumb to the temptation of excuses. Why explain everything? Most people aren't interested in our explanatory tales. They're too busy dealing with the consequences of our retraction, because it necessitates a change of plans, and often this involves additional work. Now, because of us, they need to make new arrangements and somehow fill the gap that's emerged. So, most of them don't want to be bothered with the intricacies of our justifications. It's far easier for them to accept a cancellation when it is delivered in a human, self-responsible and unambiguous manner, instead of being garnished with hollow phrases signifying fake regret.

If we clearly and concisely tell the other person how things are, the chances are that he or she won't even be angry – quite contrary to what we were expecting. Like attracts like: the rowdy the angry, the calm the quiet, and clarity begets clarity. So, if we're clear about the subject, relaxed in our tone and focused on the result, we're doing the smart thing – and not just when it comes to cancellations. A simple statement is the best way forward. 'I've changed my mind' sits well; it states what is without cumbersome explanations, and it does no one any real harm. And in the unlikely event that the person you're talking to questions your decision, you've got two other sentences to fall back on that fit very nicely here: sentence 18, 'As I said', and sentence 24, 'It all sounds logical, yet my feelings suggest something else'. Both sentences work without creating drama; they don't provoke accusations or require justification.

'I've changed my mind' works very nicely for Til. A couple of hours after talking with his client, he leaves me a voice message. 'It was really easy,' he says, sounding extremely relieved. 'He didn't even demand to know why. "It just doesn't fit" actually did the trick!'

I'm glad I get that kind of feedback regularly. It's confirmation that it's worthwhile to remain tenacious, but in a relaxed way, and enhance one's self-leadership skills. If you want to thrive, you have to create the right conditions within yourself. That's also beneficial for the people we engage with. Our fellow humans may on occasion be astounded by how easily seemingly intractable problems can be solved. And, anyway, problems aren't the problem. They're not important. What matters is how we view a supposed problem – and how we deal with it.

'I've changed my mind.' A short, casually spoken sentence that instantly puts an end to self-reproach and a guilty conscience and lets you, once again, be the person that does you good – the self-assured creator of your own destiny.

WHAT THIS SENTENCE GIVES YOU

RELIEF
FREEDOM
POWER

30

IT IS HOW IT IS
HOW IT IS

'They're casting for the main role in a new Netflix series next week, and guess who they've invited? Moi! Me, myself, I!' Hanna bellows through the phone. I can picture her literally jumping up and down for joy. 'I'll be flying to New Yooork! And before that, I'll be shooting in Scotland for two months! TWO MONTHS!!' Then she dives into all the wonderful details. 'And you, my dear, are going to be thoroughly prepping me for my red carpet appearance. Red carpet – here I come!'

I'm really happy for Hanna. And for myself: red carpet preps are always good fun. Next to the obvious things concerning appearance and visual impact, there are plenty of nuances which require a certain finesse. For instance, how to answer questions no one has asked – and I'm not referring to those appallingly obvious evasion tactics politicians like to deploy when they're being asked something. But this is all a fair way off for Hanna. First, she'll need to win the audition, negotiate a contract and, well . . . there's the small matter of actually performing in the series.

A couple of months later she finally gets that crucial

phone call. After a nail-biting shortlisting process involving ever more video calls and her getting her hopes up, the final message is that a woman from Holland got the part. The winner has blonder hair and is taller and younger, her agent says. 'What? Are you kidding me? This is all just about looks?! Ever heard of wigs, make-up, shoes?!' Hanna is beside herself.

A couple of weeks later she's still furious, so we decide to deal with the issue during a coaching session. She talks herself into a rage again, and I intervene: 'Where were you when that original call came, inviting you to the audition?'

'What? I was at the dairy shelf in the wholefoods shop – what's that got to do with it?' She doesn't like the question.

'And how were you feeling that day?'

'Good. I think.' She's trying to remember. 'I'd just been told I'd got the main role in one episode of a series; the money from another production had just come in; and I had a crush on someone. So . . . good, yeah.'

'Right,' I tell her. 'Then I'd like you to go back to that day, back to that shop. Walk along the row to where the dairy goods are. Can you do that?'

'All right,' she says, a little reluctantly, though she's closed her eyes without me having to prompt her.

'OK, now I want you to imagine you're looking at your mobile – and it doesn't ring.'

'Whaaat?'

'That's right, it simply doesn't ring, and it won't. Not in the shop and not after you've left it. Your agent isn't going to phone you. You were never offered the role. That's the new story. You don't even know the series exists.'

Hanna seems startled, eyes now wide open. Then she's suddenly very calm and it actually seems as if the space around her has got a little bit lighter.

This can happen when we're distraught and we suddenly have a flash of inspiration – when we realize, as in this case, that we're grieving because of something we've lost, when it was never ours to begin with. When this realization moves from our heads to our hearts, our negative thoughts dissolve and we feel much lighter. And then our brain is able to break the big drama down into easily digestible facts. The most important one, in Hanna's case, is that the only role she played in the story was as someone who had a chance to get a role. That's all. She hasn't lost anything because the role was never hers to lose. She felt fine in the shop. Until she got that call the role didn't mean anything at all to her.

So, if you're struggling with something like this, go back to the crossing where you turned off and, in your mind, take a different turn-off, or proceed straight ahead. A little fantasy trip, in conjunction with the mundane sentence 'It is how it is how it is', can work like a miracle. A comforting medicine for all the many opportunities we were never able to realize.

I can also highly recommend it for situations where we're plagued by guilt. For instance, the jinxed holiday phenomenon – freelancers will instantly know what I mean. For weeks, you haven't had a commission. Your last holiday was ages ago. Temptation gets the better of you. And the moment you leave there's a flood of job offers. Performers especially seem beset by this rendition of Murphy's law. What to do if you're sitting on a beach and a lucrative engagement pops up – a photoshoot, a film role, a mega project? If it's too late, let it go. Instantly. Accept, relinquish, acknowledge – whatever word calms you the most. 'It is how it is how it is', as a little monologue, can quickly sort things out. Some may find this too fatalistic, like a capitulation. Here's another way of viewing it: as an invitation to adopt a more relaxed attitude which will save you a great deal of energy.

If the opportunity has passed, the top job is gone, the estate agent has a different buyer, the last flight has left – take it easy. Calm down, breathe in, breathe out. Realize that it is how it is how it is. And that it's completely pointless to obsess about something you can't change. Leaving the past where it belongs is the best way forward anyway. 'There are only two days in the year where nothing can be done,' as the Dalai Lama succinctly put it. 'One is called yesterday and the other is called tomorrow.'

And if you *can* still change things? When something is bothering you, but you can still influence the outcome? In an instance like this, anger or frustration – normally negative emotions – can be channelled to achieve something positive. They can give you the thrust and enthusiasm you need to have a second go at something.

The Serenity Prayer is a wise reminder that we always have a choice over how to react to things: 'Grant me the serenity to accept the things I cannot change, courage to change the things I can, and wisdom to know the difference.' So true, so easy, so hard. If we could all just forever manage that . . .

*

So, what about Hanna? Four months later she knew why not getting the role was actually a blessing in disguise: on a different production – one she had been able to do because she hadn't been chosen for the Netflix series – she met the man of her dreams. They've been married for a couple of years. The wedding invitation had a little proverb embossed on it in gold lettering: 'It is how it is how it is'.

CALMNESS
RELIEF
PEACE

Radio B Zwei's *See You Later* – the dating show where listeners get to know listeners! Every Saturday evening on 92.4, with Karin Kuschik. Steffen is on the line. He's forty-two, lives in Potsdam and would like to be in a relationship again before winter starts.

'Hi, Steffen.'

'Hi, Karin.'

'So, tell me, what do you reckon is one of your defining characteristics, on which all your friends would agree – you know, that's typically Steffen? What comes to mind?'

Without hesitation, he says: 'I'm incorruptible.'

Incorruptible? I don't think anyone has ever answered this question claiming incorruptibility as an attribute before. 'Sounds interesting. Give me an example,' I respond, and Steffen tells me how he recently turned down a colleague's invitation to her birthday party with the words 'I don't think that'll work, really, but thanks.' Confused, she prompted him: 'You mean, you can't make it on that day?' 'No, I mean, we're just not compatible.' Wow. She didn't know how to respond. After all, it's not the sort of remark you hear every day.

The programme assistant, aghast, is staring at me through the soundproof studio window, and the sound engineer looks up from his newspaper.

'I can imagine that kind of statement doesn't always go down well,' I say to Steffen.

'Sure, a lot of people think it's rude, but no offence is intended,' the incorruptible Steffen answers. 'It's just a fact that some people don't really fit together, isn't it? I mean, it's no big deal, it's not a judgement about the other person.'

'It isn't?' I ask, somewhat astounded. I can see the assistant and the sound engineer staring at each other in the control room.

'Not at all,' says Steffen. 'I mean, you wouldn't try on a shirt if it wasn't your style.'

Interesting comparison. Fair enough, though, and it says less about the quality of the shirt than the person who won't wear it.

That's the fun of live broadcasting: just as you're settling into your mental business-as-usual routine, something surprising happens and you get a rush of adrenalin. The drawback is: limited time. The clock is telling me to hurry. The news is coming up at 8.30 and I have to fit a song, advertising and a traffic report into the three and a half minutes I have until then. Sorry, Steffen, it was nice talking to you.

'We're just not compatible.' How unflustered that can sound if you just say it naturally – without an attitude, without reproach, in a calm tone of voice. Am I seriously recommending this sentence as a good way to decline a birthday invitation? Hardly. But, within the plethora of responses we generally have at our disposal, I do think this sentence worthy of consideration.

It would certainly save many couples a lot of misery, though admittedly it might mean that their relationship would be short. Because, we often persuade ourselves that people, or circumstances, match our expectations, rather than listening to that subtle inner voice that regretfully but clearly advises you to say: 'We're just not compatible. We're not doing each other any good. Let's not take it any further.' But who has the courage to say that?

Some people have never learnt to say 'no'. When an opportunity arises, there's an uninvited inner censor who pronounces: 'You can't possibly say that!' Thus, we force ourselves to spend time with someone because our impulse to say 'yes' was stronger than our desire to make a calm, realistic assessment of the situation: do I even like this person? Does it do me good to meet up with him or her? After we've met, do I feel exhausted or more alive, annoyed or full of energy? These are all important questions when it comes to living a fulfilled life. And some people fit together, while others don't. So, if you're able to say, with heartfelt honesty, 'Thank you for your good intentions, I just don't think we're compatible', you'll probably save yourself a lot of trouble.

Of course, this makes us feel uncomfortable; saying 'yes' would be so much easier, because we don't want to disappoint people, or we simply don't wish to offend. Even our ego prefers this option, because – as in the case of Steffen and the birthday party – an invitation means our presence is appreciated, and of course that's flattering. And so we engage with people who cost us valuable time and don't enrich our hearts.

This ambivalence also extends to material things. Think of all the walnut oils, vases, candleholders, cookbooks and socks we've been given in the course of our lives, that we have never used. How many of us have raved about the scratchy scarf we were given as a present that we have no intention of ever wearing? We don't wish to cause offence, so we lie to ourselves. Fake joy, rather than honest astonishment, seems to be the standard response. Because we never learnt to say: 'Thanks, but no thanks.'

It's worth striving to overcome this reluctance, or the fear of giving an authentic response. When we do, we soon realize we've been dealing with a phantom. In other words, being honest is easier than we think, and our effort is quickly rewarded. 'Thank you for the lovely idea, that's really nice. It's just that, it isn't my thing at all.' That may seem like an impossible thing to say, but it's usually well received. 'I think the bracelet is really pretty, I just never wear one.' The person on the receiving end of this statement is unlikely to feel offended. And the statement is true. We might like a painting, but have no desire to hang it up in our home. We enjoy some things more at a distance, when we don't have to live with them.

The other day, a client of mine had a huge row with his colleague. They had planned to start a project together, but their brainstorming session turned into a heated exchange where both parties basically accused each other of being different. 'Totally childish,' my client later conceded. And he was right. When we feel like we're not being understood, we tend to become like children. Adults wouldn't shout at each other because their mentalities are different – especially not in a business context. At some point, my client said, he suddenly had a flash of inspiration, promptly interrupted himself and proclaimed: 'You know what? We're just not compatible. That's just how it is.' There was a stunned silence. Then he continued: 'It would make more sense to make a list of what your talents are, the ones I lack, and vice versa. Then we'll know how we can move forward with this. That's the only thing that might work.' That ironed things out and they both continued calmly from then on, without feeling the need to jump down each other's throats. Who would have thought?

'Life lasts but six years. After that, it's all repetition,' a wise man once said to me. Meaning: during our first six years we have so many experiences, so many synaptic connections are forged and nerve pathways formed, that we establish important patterns for our behaviours and beliefs. After this time we basically go through a long chain of repetitions. Unfortunately, we're not aware of this. That's why, when we're engaging with others, it's worthwhile paying close attention to what is really going on. Is it actually about the *other* person, or am I unhappy because *I'm* once again experiencing something that I have found terrible on the hundred previous occasions I have experienced it? In which case: welcome to your own story.

'We're just not compatible' can be a wonderfully effective insight into many situations, whether you actually articulate this thought or keep it to yourself. It doesn't require us to change the other person, or ourselves. Rather, it prompts us to ask: which actions might be required to make our lives easier? That's the beauty of this simple, straightforward sentence. It means no offence, and it causes no offence. If you just say it in an offhand manner, it even has an innocent ring to it. Isn't it amazing, the things you can learn from dating shows . . .

I never did find out if the *See You Later* radio show helped Steffen find a suitable partner. But twenty years later his sentence 'We're just not compatible' has made it into this book. Thanks, Steffen!

WHAT THIS SENTENCE GIVES YOU

SELF-DETERMINATION

INTEGRITY

FREEDOM

32

I'D RATHER SPEND TIME WITH MYSELF RIGHT NOW

A full, deep sound echoes through the yoga studio. The gong is the signal that Shavasana has ended and, thus, my Kundalini yoga session – always a great way to start off a Sunday morning. Silently, and still a little bit dazed, we roll up our yoga mats and get into line in front of the artfully sculpted sliding doors behind which the belts and blankets are stored. And now for a nice cup of yogi tea, I'm thinking, when a screeching noise cuts through the stillness. 'Kaaaarin!' someone calls from behind me. I'm hoping they mean someone else, but I turn round just the same. Nope – unfortunately she means me.

Yvonne, a woman I briefly met during a tap dance course about seven years earlier, and who I haven't seen since, is skipping towards me. She looks amazing, and has been working as a model in advertising for years. 'Wow! Great to see you! How are you? Where have you been? What have you been up to? Do you still tap dance? I don't, any more – pity, it could have been really successful, but you know how it is . . .' While I'm wondering whether I actually do know how it is, she's already talking about her kids, but then manages to segue into the topic of castings. I'm relieved she doesn't seem to expect me to contribute anything to this 'conversation', but just as I'm thinking this, she says: 'We simply must meet up somewhere!'

'Hmm . . . must we?' I ask myself. But I don't actually say anything, because after an hour and a half of Kundalini yoga my system is still a little slow to react to the world around me. Yvonne is staring at me, expectantly. 'Go on, say something!' a tugging inner voice insists, but all I manage to do is smile and make a noise that could be interpreted as a positive signal: 'Hmm . . .'

That's all she needs. 'Great! That's what we'll do! Still got the same phone number?'

'Yep.'

'Perfect! Look, I've got to rush – the nanny's waiting. Did I tell you my boyfriend and I split up? No? I'll tell you about it, then. Ciao!' And off she runs.

I go and drink my yogi tea in silence and think about this encounter. It rarely happens to me that I'm verbally assaulted by someone who's practically a stranger, whom I've never met privately before. This is a woman who feels that is all the more reason to meet and catch up with everything that's happened during the last few years. My feeling is: now I remember why I never had the urge to meet up with her in the first place. Not the sort of thing one would say, and not something I want to say. It would be hurtful and unnecessary. All the same, I'm entitled to clarify where I stand. But how best to go about it?

I remembered a client who had a similar experience, a few years earlier, and couldn't think of an adequate way to handle it. My advice to him – surprise, surprise – was to formulate I-messages. If you want to make a statement that doesn't hurt the other person, messages about ourselves are the best. They always work, and in the case of Yvonne it obviously wouldn't be 'I don't want to meet up with you', although it would be true enough. My alternative: 'I'd rather spend time with myself right now' – which is equally true. People are usually surprised when they don't appear in our sentences – we've already touched on the topic. But that's precisely why they're never seen as an attack, and the reason they're so well received. It worked for my client. And it works with Yvonne. She promptly sends me this upbeat text message: 'I totally understand! Good on you, for expressing it that way – I have phases like that too.' So, Yvonne left my orbit again.

There are some positive side-effects to getting older. You become more relaxed about things, I find. When I was thirty, I wouldn't have dared to say something like that to Yvonne. I'd have spent an entire evening with her without really knowing why. In a way, I would have been disloyal to myself, and if I was really unlucky this muddled beginning might have mutated into a lengthy relationship, of sorts. Not good. It's rarely happened to me, but it has happened nevertheless. In fact, I've had my fill. Are you familiar with these kinds of relationships?

As far as values are concerned, I'm fairly old-school: reliability, commitment, respect, punctuality – I think all these are good and important things. I just realized, this sounds very German, and very boring. But that's the way it is. These values tend to conflict with much cooler ones, such as tolerance and a laissez-faire approach to life, and this can be challenging. So, along the way, I started adopting something that is totally at odds with my values: noncommitment. I call it my homeopathic dose (we'll come to that!).

My role models are from a different generation. I find it extraordinary how casually people in their, say, mid-twenties cope in the absence of values I've always held to. There seems to be a causal relationship between age and the extent of noncommitment. I'll try to explain what I mean, using the same situation across four generations.

For people in their seventies or eighties, 'next Wednesday, at 3.30 p.m.' means next Wednesday, at 3.30 p.m. There are no two ways about it – an agreement is an agreement. The host buys his or her favourite cake from the bakery on Wednesday morning to ensure it'll be on the table at 3.30 p.m. And, at what time do the guests ring the doorbell? That's right: Wednesday, at 3.30 p.m.

A generation later, 'Wednesday, at 3.30 p.m.' means you phone on Tuesday evening to confirm: 'Is it still on, at 3.30, tomorrow?' It's basically a leading question, but they just want to be certain. The cake is bought a couple of hours earlier; coffee, tea or water is at hand and ready to be served.

Generation Y. Same day, in the morning, a WhatsApp: '3.30 still on?' Reply: 'Sure.' There's probably no cake, but whatever can be found in the kitchen is placed on the table. And the automatic coffee machine is switched on when the visitors arrive: 'Coffee? Cappuccino? Espresso? Strong, weak – on a scale from four to eleven? Decaf?' If someone ordered an Americano with brown sugar, that would be fine too. Millennials can handle this sort of thing with ease.

Gen Z. At 3.35 p.m., there's a voice message with a lot of background noise: 'Running late.' Reply: 'No sweat.'

Smiling face with sweat emoji. Friends arrive at four, bringing their own drinks in climate-friendly bottles. No snacks!

I know, this is all totally cliché. Then again, generalizations are based on shared experiences of roughly the same things, and they make categorization easier.

So, what does all this have to do with the sentence 'I'd rather spend time with myself right now'? Nothing, and everything. As a classic red line, or demarcation statement, it's an invitation to a self-determined life. And, since setting boundaries becomes easier when we do it with a clear conscience, these Wednesday-at-3.30-p.m. stories have hidden within them clues to a little tool I call a homeopathic dose. Its application is simple. Think of an attitude that totally contradicts your values – in my case, noncommittal babble. Then take a mini dose of this attitude to spruce up the undertaking you find difficult – in my case, calmly cancelling Yvonne. The result: it becomes much easier.

Life is too precious to spend with people we don't care about, to talk about things that don't enrich us. So, the ability to cancel charmingly is simply a no-brainer if you want to make your life easier.

WHAT THIS SENTENCE GIVES YOU

TIME

SELF-RESPECT

CLARITY

33

I TRULY UNDERSTAND

I'm in the middle of the previous chapter, and my laptop suddenly crashes. For a couple of seconds the image on the screen goes fuzzy, like one of those ancient television sets where you had to adjust the aerial. Then it goes black. OK, no problem: I'll just reboot using that savvy key-combination thingy for which you need three hands – hey, yoga's got to be good for something ;-) But even that doesn't help, and my digital friend remains schtum. As this is a six-month-old pro model with all the bells and whistles, I'm confident the problem can be solved relatively easily by calling the hotline. In my experience, crashes that can't be fixed by standard first-aid measures aren't user-fixable (not without help, anyway), and I'm reckoning on a two-hour hotline pit stop before I'm back on track and working again.

It soon turns out that my faith was misplaced. The crash was just the first act of a lengthy drama. When I finally manage to locate the hotline number it turns out to be so hot, I'm kicked off the line. On my second attempt I have to navigate through a long list of options before being told that, in my case, I need to call a different number. After a few listless conversations, during which I'm asked to describe the problem again and again, I'm told to drive to the supplier's main outlet to let the on-site service team tackle the issue. But this, I'm informed, might be difficult because I don't have an appointment – I might have to wait till tomorrow. Whaaat?! I jump in my car and head for the outlet on Berlin's Ku'damm – where there's a will, there's a way!

I'm assuming you've had similar experiences with repair services – computers, fridges, routers . . . different devices, same story. So I'll skip some of the inane details; we've all heard the phrases: 'can't be done . . . it was always like this . . . my hands are tied . . . company policy . . . it'll take time . . . have to send it in . . . I really can't say'. Long story short, I tell the service team person that I can't afford not to work for ten days, and I'm told: 'If you want to continue writing, you'll need to buy a new laptop.' Great. Wasn't the one I had already virtually new? And, how about hiring them out? The good news, from today's perspective: if my laptop does crash again, I've got a spanking new one at home to replace it with.

It's only when I do my evening routine that I realize what was missing on this day. I love these little check-ins with myself, to say farewell to the day in an appropriate way. So, on laptop-crash day I did my Evening Check, consisting of three questions for an attentive mind, so that the body can sleep better. First question: what disturbed me that day? Answer: lack of understanding, or empathy – in every single conversation. None of the people I talked to – people who, surely, have been trained to do their jobs – demonstrated any kind of personal engagement, something like 'I completely understand' or 'I'm sorry, that must be really awkward for you'. That would have helped, because it feels so much better when you're not just talking but being taken seriously. And before I get to question number two I'm already asleep.

Sometimes, when my make-the-world-a-better-place impulse gets the better of me, I'll actively promote the notion that empathy vastly improves interpersonal communication. The other day, for instance, when the lady from the glazing company calls to say that they'll need to come round a fourth time because someone has forgotten something again. Four appointments for the same window – really? When the woman stubbornly refuses to utter a single word of regret, I inform her that more understanding on her part would make the conversation a lot more pleasant for me. How about: 'I understand it's awkward for you to have to make time for this again, sorry about the inconvenience' – anything, really, that would suggest there is a human being on the *other* end of the line who understands what it's like on *this* end of the line. The lady from the glazing company is not pleased with my suggestion. She screams something about me not being the only client and hangs up. While I'm still staring at the phone, dumbfounded, I can't help thinking, 'I hope that never happens to you if you need to dial 999,' and I'm imagining the scene: 'Do you think you're the only person who's just had a heart attack?!' Switching perspectives – always a worthwhile exercise.

Of course, I can understand why customer service staff, of all people, are reluctant to engage with the distress of their clientele: they want to defuse it by guiding us away from the problem, towards a solution. From a psychological vantage point, however, I suspect that many are simply overtaxed. If your job involves being permanently inundated with complaints, accusations, people asking the exact same questions and moaning about why in this particular case they can't possibly do without their laptop 'because otherwise I can't do my job!', you definitely need to learn how to distance yourself, or you start to go numb. Initiate self-defence mechanisms, raise the drawbridge, say your lines, list the options, stay friendly. That's the maximum when you're constantly confronted with distress and anger. I think that's only human. The problem is it's not good enough.

A note of empathy, a brief focus on what the person is really saying; then a step back to establish the necessary boundary – that would be so much more effective. I realize that's not a natural impulse when you're locked in your own story and you don't feel you have the capacity for other people's worries – that's true on both sides. Nevertheless, it is especially true that people whose job it is to listen to complaints truly benefit from a willingness to switch perspectives. And the next time you're in a situation where you find this quality lacking in the person you're talking to, here's an active way to get yourself that much-needed dose of empathy: 'I'd be happy if you briefly put yourself in my situation. How would you feel if you experienced this? What would you like to hear if you were me, now?' A little nudge that opens up new possibilities. And, yes, sometimes – as was the case with the lady from the glazing company – they'll hang up on you.

Life gets easier when we remember that the other person probably wants the same thing we do: understanding. 'I really understand how you must feel' is a reliable way to break the ice, a signal for de-escalation. It's worth keeping in mind, because isn't that how meaningful conversations always begin – accepting that the other person might be right?

And, at other times, it isn't even about understanding, we just want to be heard, acknowledged. It makes us instantly feel better. We know this from children. A little girl might cry because the holiday's over, her best friend is wearing the same dress, or her guinea pig has died. Grown-ups often try to comfort using reason, or they say: 'You don't have to cry.' As if any child that ever lived has ever reacted to this by drying their tears, nodding and saying: 'It's true, it's pointless, I'd better stop. Thanks for the tip.'

And, as adults, when we're het-up we don't need rational tips either. Because when we're emotionally charged, when we think the world is being unfair to us, our inner child has already taken over. And when we're in this state of being about five years old, what we need is reassurance. We want to be heard, hugged, and for someone to sort everything out. So, in these moments it's a blessing when someone just understands us. And, of course, it's as much of a bless-ing when we can do the same for others. 'I truly understand' has a fast and reliably soothing effect on those agitated, childish elements inside us.

WHAT THIS SENTENCE GIVES YOU

UNDERSTANDING

WILLINGNESS TO TALK

EMPATHY

34

I WISH I COULD BE
HAPPIER FOR YOU

I love coaching actors. They're incredibly inquisitive and, as such, they're a wonderful counterpart to my experiences in the corporate world. They seem to have an intrinsic interest in personal growth and a bold willingness to go beyond their comfort zones – which might explain why they were drawn to the profession. It's a joy to work with them because we can cover a lot of ground quickly, or take an in-depth look at just one topic. They don't need convincing – they have already made the choice to engage with themselves before deciding to get coaching. Always an ideal place to start.

If you're a corporate client reading these lines and have, with lightning speed and great decisiveness, deduced that the opposite must be true of you, please, hold your horses. Working with business execs also has great advantages – such as their ability to make these kinds of conclusive, lightning-quick inferences! It's simply that, in this particular story, the focus is on performing artists.

Most actors lean towards to self-contemplation, which in turn necessitates a degree of honesty about oneself. Both are useful in their profession. Emotional intelligence is another quality that is often highly developed in actors. Unfortunately, envy and resentment often cancel out the positive qualities. Unlike in most other professions, actors automatically compare themselves with colleagues. It's probably inevitable. As soon as they see someone in a role they also find compelling, an inner questionnaire unfolds. How would *I* have cast the character? What would it do for my image if I were able to play a role in a certain way? Would it be a useful addition for my demo tape? How can I get to know that amazing director? Would I have been more convincing in that role? Why wasn't I invited to the casting? How come I was there, but didn't get a part? Is it time to get a different agent? So many questions.

Never-ending pressure to improve and optimize; endless comparisons. A chimney sweep probably wouldn't have these concerns. Or a heart surgeon, or a plumber, or a dental technician. Certainly I don't as a coach, because I'll never know what other coaches achieve in a face-to-face session – unless I book one for myself. This permanent state of comparing is unique to artists, especially actors, because we're inundated with films and videos, wherever we are.

Although most actors surely know it's the fastest route into a personal drama, most of them do it – and inevitably lose, against others or against themselves. They get themselves on to dangerous terrain where their only choice is between two highly unattractive options, or poles. On the one end there's arrogance, loathing and resentment. That can sound like this: 'God, she was bad! I would have done it better, without a day's preparation.' Or there's the polar opposite, where uncertainty, self-destructiveness and disappointment prevail: 'I should pack it in! She's ten times better than me. I'm too old, too big, too small, too fat, too thin, too intelligent for this kind of work.'

It's amazing how, on the one hand, actors support each other with tips about castings, photographers, workshops, coachings. They'll exchange contacts, help fellow actors look good in front of the camera, give helpful feedback. And yet . . . There's this nasty stinging sensation when a colleague gets the part, when a friend lands a three-page spread in a celebrity magazine, when the photographers around the red carpet shout someone else's name louder than theirs.

By the way, I'm not referring to the Kate Winslets, Brad Pitts, Kristen Stewarts and Daniel Craigs of this world, those five per cent of actors and actresses everyone knows, and for whom the situation is surely quite different. I am talking about all those incredible talents who have always given their best, without many people noticing. And those are clearly the majority.

German Film Awards, Berlin, late in the evening (at least I think it was, as I remember that some of the women already had their high heels in their hands, rather than on their feet). Near the bistro table where I'm waiting with two glasses of prosecco, two women have plonked themselves on the stairs, heaving a sigh of relief. One of them has a golden Lola award jutting proudly out of her handbag – for the best female main role of the year. Both women are in the same league, the winner is perhaps a tad more famous.

'You know what?' the Lola-less actress says, 'I wish I could be happier for you.'

Her companion looks startled. 'What do you mean?'

'I wish I could feel happier for you,' she says again. 'But it won't work, even though I'm trying.' Silence. Then, with a steady gaze, she adds: 'Nonetheless, and from my heart – congratulations!'

'Thank you,' the Lola-winner says, taking the award out of her handbag. 'That means a lot to me.' Inspecting it, she adds: 'I deserved it, didn't I?'

'That's true,' says the other actress, and then, after a pause: 'Me too, though.'

'That's true,' says the winner, and hands her the statuette.

Now both of them are smiling.

A calm, honest and authentic scene I just happened to witness. Quite a feat. And I mean for both women.

What impressed me about the sentence? It was real, and it pre-empted that hollow, fake display of joy. Don't the others know who is envious or resentful anyway? When they don't look you in the eye, when their tone is a tad too jolly; giveaway words creep in, like '*Honestly*, I'm *really* happy for you!' Really? How much classier it would be to just keep the envy where it belongs: with oneself. Always a good opportunity for some self-reflection.

'Wow, congratulations!' my friend Mark once said to Philipp, both of them music producers. We've all known each other for years, and the two of them like each other a lot. That day it became clear that not only had Philipp's single hit the charts before Mark's, he'd also sold more than half a million copies. 'That's great,' said Mark. 'I just wish I could be happier for you. I mean, platinum, for God's sake!' There it was again, that sentence. And because Mark's strong point is honesty, he added, 'I guess I'll have to work on the shared joy thing,' and everyone laughed. Being able to admit it in that way had a liberating quality. Just listening to him felt like a relief.

So, if you happen to experience that nasty stinging sensation at some point, while someone else has all the luck in the world, you might like either of these little stories. You don't even have to actually say the sentence – it's enough to think the counter-proposal, as a kind of softly spoken monologue: 'What a thing, I'm really not able to feel happy for the other person. I can do better than that!' Just taking stock of where you stand can release a lot of negative energy. Energy which you might otherwise have unfairly wielded against the joyful winner. And that really wouldn't do anyone any good.

'I wish I could be happier for you.' A statement of self-reflection and generosity. A sentence that can instantly make two people's lives easier. Solutions can be that simple.

WHAT THIS SENTENCE GIVES YOU
INSIGHT
HONESTY
CLASS

35
I WOULD NEVER GIVE YOU THE PRIVILEGE

once interviewed an Indian guru. He was a yogi, a speaker, an author, a mystic . . . and, apparently, he excelled at everything he did. This man had more followers than Switzerland has residents. His vision: inner transformation for everyone, as a normal part of everyday life, like brushing your teeth. Your daily soul-hygiene, so to speak. And his promise was to teach everyone the effective techniques that are necessary for this. I found that interesting.

To launch his book in Germany, his team decide on a talk-show format, on a large stage. As presenters, apart from myself, they have chosen an actress and moderator who has done her homework. So, between us, we have plenty of good questions to put to the guru. But, somehow, it's hard to get a conversation going. Perhaps because he's accustomed to speaking *to* people rather than *with* them. At any rate, I can't see how his answers have a lot to do with our questions, and, of course, it's part of a moderator's job to point this out. Under normal circumstances this would be an easy task, but if you're sitting across from a high-ranking guru in a long white robe, with a beautifully tied turban and a long white beard, and this person is regarded as a spiritually enlightened figure, well . . . it's not quite that easy. I interrupt him anyway, stating clearly that I'm conscious of my transgression – that seems appropriate.

So, what happened? Put it this way: a harmonious atmosphere feels different. My verbal rugby tackle is answered with two seconds of deafening silence. The energy in the room definitely has an edge. When several thousand people are shocked, it can feel like a punch to your stomach. To bring some lightness to the situation, I turn my head to the audience and say, nonchalantly, 'Oops! Did I just insult the guru?' People start to breathe again, I can see smiles. I'm smiling too. Even the guru is smiling. But, it's also clear that an unspoken rule has been broken, a rule which states 'Only speak when the master has finished talking' and not 'Interrupt him whenever you feel like it'. So, he's smiling – smugly, I would say. And with a determined glint in his eyes. Then he says: 'I would never give you the privilege to insult me.'

Ouch.

Another of those magical sentences that, just for an instant, have the power to stop time. To my mind, it was the most important sentence of his entire appearance that day.

The power propelling this message and the self-assurance of its delivery encompass everything that is important to me in life and in coaching: self-leadership, the ability to reflect, awareness, self-worth and self-confidence. The smugness? OK, that was unnecessary. But this sentence has a similar potency to the opening sentence of this book: 'I decide who pushes my buttons.' Here, too, the core of it has to do with status. How much power, or control, do I allow someone to have over me? Should another person really be permitted to determine how I feel? Do I want others to control my life? If these questions were put to us in a neutral situation – say, we were given a questionnaire – I'm certain that everyone in the world would give the same answers: 'Very little' and 'No'. Of course we don't want to give others control over us. They shouldn't be allowed to determine what I think. Whether I'm angry, lie awake at night, or I'm desperate – those are my decisions. Most sane individuals would agree. Better to act autonomously than to allow others to do what they wish with us. In theory.

In practice, we still find ourselves saying things like 'You're the reason I feel bad', 'You've made me feel really nervous', 'If you look at me that way, it's no wonder I feel insecure'. Unfortunately, when someone is poking our most sensitive trigger points, sentences like these seem to be true. At those moments, our human know-how fails, and sometimes we forget that we are responsible for our feelings. Of course, others can try to rattle us, but, luckily, the decision lies with us. Particularly in challenging situations, it's good to remember that we can always freely choose how we want to react to the world around us, and what we wish to think.

'Die Gedanken sind frei' ('Thoughts Are Free') is an old German folksong, and it's no coincidence that it was popular in times of political oppression. For example, when Sophie Scholl's father was thrown in jail by the Nazis for criticizing Hitler, his daughter would stand outside the prison walls every evening and play the song on her recorder. It must have been very moving, hearing this innocent little tune with its mighty message drift over the prison wall and into his cell.

Thoughts *are* free. That's why we can always choose whether we want to feel attacked, or not – regardless of whether someone is actually attacking us. 'I would never give you the privilege to insult me' succinctly demonstrates this attitude in a no-fuss and confident manner. The sentence can easily be adapted to different situations. 'I hope I haven't insulted you?' 'No, I'd never give you the privilege', or 'Not to worry, you don't have that privilege.' A convincing reaction which, in combination with a genuine smile, can even come across as charming rather than arrogant, and still convey a generous measure of self-determination. Sentences like these have the power to give us a feeling of inner strength, even if we're not yet convinced that what we are saying is completely true. In such instances, the classic formula 'Fake it till you make it' applies. In other words: say it anyway. If your ears hear a strong message coming from you, the message will soon feel true on the inside too. It works both ways: new and clear statements can change our attitude, and a new attitude can prompt us to express ourselves more clearly, without even thinking about it.

What other people think of us depends, to a large extent, on what we think of ourselves. Another good reason to be clear about our beliefs. 'I would never give you the privilege' is a sentence well worth remembering to remind yourself that no one but you has the power to determine how you feel.

WHAT THIS SENTENCE GIVES YOU

SELF-DETERMINATION
SUPREME CONFIDENCE
INVIOLABILITY

36

I THINK I'LL JUST
TAKE *THIS*

—

I'm one of those spontaneous decision-makers. It wasn't always like that. There was a time when, if I was in a restaurant, by the time I was ready to order I'd know the menu by heart – and even then I'd hesitate. It would drive my fellow diners mad. That's why, out of pure respect for their time and grumbling stomachs, I, for once, made a spontaneous decision. I decided to get rid of this nervy cocktail of hesitation, uncertainty and speculation. Joining Team Decisive was a much more appealing prospect. When I consider how difficult I imagined this change to be and how easy it actually was, I call it the diving board phenomenon. You stand there for ages, jittering on the edge of the platform, waiting for the right moment. Yet, the difference between waiting and jumping is, in the end, just one small step. It takes less than a second. And when we finally do it it is not because our fear has miraculously disappeared. Rather, something inside us has understood that courage doesn't mean you're not afraid any more. Courage means being afraid but doing it anyway. It's about making a decision. And that's what this chapter addresses.

To be clear, if you're someone who enjoys endlessly comparing online reviews and pores over catalogues to decide whether to order your new kitchen with an oak or walnut veneer, you might like to skip this chapter. You might also want to do so if you're a rapid decision-maker – unless you'd like to find out how the rest of the world ticks. But if you happen to be someone who suffers from irresoluteness, who would rather stop wasting time and move from dithering to doing but doesn't know how to, given the many choices, this chapter is for you. Here's your chance to strike a fundamental deal with yourself: to decide what you want when you can't make up your mind. Sounds crazy? It isn't.

I'm offering you an exit strategy for situations which usually trigger a debilitating cascade of thoughts. As soon as you notice you might be drifting into this state, here's an inconspicuous, magical little sentence which will instantly solve the conundrum: 'I think I'll just take *this*.' It's so banal you might almost think it trite, yet it's extremely effective, and, as with so many insights, it's resulted from a key experience.

A Tex-Mex restaurant at the beginning of the 1990s. Back then, they seemed to be everywhere in Berlin, with their obligatory neon cacti. You could smell cheese sauce everywhere, and people who couldn't manage a single 'gracias' during their vacation could say jalapeño as if they'd never eaten anything else. To this day I'm not sure I'm that keen on Tex-Mex, but, like turkey or a nut roast at Xmas, and chocolate eggs at Easter, it's become a staple.

One of the capital's most popular examples has fine sand covering its floor and a Yucatán beach feel. Just as I'm trying to level my table on the sandy floor, I overhear a short conversation at a neighbouring table that immediately changes my life.

'You always order the first best thing that catches your eye,' a man complains to his companion, a woman with a black micro-pony haute-couture-cum-punk hairdo and a Snow White complexion. He's clearly stressed, because she's already ordered and he's having to endure the waitress's impatient gaze.

'Of course I take the first best thing. Would you rather I take the second best?' Snow White says, nonchalantly.

I'm astounded. The possibilities hinted at in this statement are immediately apparent to me, quite apart from the cheeky humour.

I'm reminded of my childhood. Our mothers didn't hand us a menu when we got home from school – I would eat what was being cooked, and, if I was unlucky, that might be fried liver. In those days we'd never have been able to imagine all the hype around the topic of food in the twenty-first century. We were light years away from the pressure we have today to constantly make decisions. It starts in the morning, when we visit a coffee shop: 'Normal or decaf? Single, double, triple? Regular milk, lactose-free, almond, oat or soya milk? Whole, non-fat, semi-skimmed? Hot/cold? Own cup, refill or cardboard?' And that's just the coffee. It's bizarre the number of decisions you're asked to make before it's even 9 a.m. – additionally frustrating for people who have trouble making up their minds.

So, how about taking it easy and behaving like the woman in the restaurant? Or, like me: since hearing this sentence I usually, and simply, just order the first best thing. As soon as I see something that appeals to me I close the menu – in the figurative sense as well. From choosing a dish to selecting wallpaper to going on holiday ... First best? Over in this corner, please! What a relief it is, and an improvement for one's quality of life.

Here's an example. You're unsure which of the trousers you've just tried on you want to buy. The quickest way out of the conundrum would be to remember this chapter, point to one of them and say: 'I think I'll just take *this*!' If it's the right decision, you'll immediately feel it. And all the more so if it's wrong. Sometimes you might not feel it until the next morning, when you want to wear the trousers and it doesn't feel right; when reluctance and regret suddenly swell up inside you. In that case, simply follow the advice given under sentence 22: '"I'm not sure" always means "no".' So, you go back to the shop.

Changing course in this way is completely legitimate, and in a case like this it's even desirable. After all, this defiant 'Yes, but ...' sensation was especially sent by your intuition so you can feel what needs to be done. That's precisely the challenge the indecisive face: they never get a proper feeling for something because all these pros and cons are constantly blocking the way. If you'd like to experience it differently in future, my suggestion is that you strike a binding deal with yourself. The next time that I-don't-know-what-to-do feeling creeps up on you, just choose anything, whatever it is: left or right, black or white, Costa Rica or Costa Brava. It doesn't matter. Because it's not the decision that really matters in your case, it's the reaction to the decision. That's the eye-opener: your feeling. Why not try it out? And don't wait until the next big decision needs to be made: start with the small things, where there's less at stake. Choose a neutral moment and make a solemn oath to yourself. It works.

Sometimes it's also helpful to realize that a decision *for* something is automatically a decision *against* everything else. If I say 'yes' to this one man, I'm saying 'no' to a million others. If I order this e-bike, I'm saying no to all the others on offer. If you choose menu number 103, there are 102 dishes you won't be eating today. It's as simple as that. If, instead, you continue to cast your mind across the vast range of alternatives, the chances are you'll despair, because you're living in a constant state of limbo, driven by the illusion that there is a perfect solution. As a committed perfectionist, let me tell you: there are always alternatives, even in the realm of perfection. So: 'I think I'll just take *this . . .*'

To do or not to do? Pondering isn't an option. There you go, another formula to make life easier. It's simply healthier to say to yourself: only doubt when it's really necessary. And, otherwise, have faith.

WHAT THIS SENTENCE GIVES YOU

SAFETY
FREEDOM
A LOT OF TIME

37

YES, FORTUNATELY

'Does this hurt?' the friendly orthopaedic surgeon asks me as he presses the lump on my wrist. 'Ouch!' is my indignant response, before I can think of something better to say. He nods empathically, types something into his computer and proceeds to move the lump backwards and forwards with his fingers. 'There's movement there, so that's good.'

'If you need surgery done on your hand, it's got to be *that* hospital,' my orthopaedist had insisted. 'And if you go there, it's *got* to be their chief surgeon. He's *the* specialist when it comes to hand surgery.' 'Easy for him to say,' is what I thought. 'He's not paying for it.' But I made an appointment anyway. A right-handed person's right hand? Only the best will do. 'The lump I removed was the size of an egg,' the hand surgeon will tell me a few weeks later. But we don't know that yet.

'We'll only know exactly what it is when we send it to the lab,' my surgeon-to-be tells me, and pushes a brown envelope containing X-ray images across the table. 'The MRI

CD is in there too,' he says, and then more seriously: 'Hand surgery is always a bit complicated, and that's a very intricate area – a lot joins up in there.' He throws me a long, meaningful gaze.

If that was meant to sound encouraging, it failed. I'm about to leave when I realize I'm losing my composure, because I suddenly say, straight out: 'But you *do* know what you're doing?' He looks up, I look down, both of us astonished. I try to take the edge off by adding: 'I mean, the operation. You can do it really, really well, right?'

He chuckles, and then beams at me, and I can see there's no ego involved when he answers: 'Yes, fortunately!' All my doubts are instantly dissipated and I immediately calm down. I'm impressed, too. Fortunately? What a brief, happy, confident answer. One to remember, and a phrase that would have been extremely useful on so many occasions.

When I started out as a coach, I was often confronted with a great deal of scepticism: 'Have you ever coached a patent lawyer?' 'How can you conduct a workshop when you don't know the ins and outs of the steel industry?' 'How much do you know about audit and assurance? After all, you'll be coaching our auditors.' Back in those days, I was a bit startled. How could an understanding of IFRS 9 be important for successful sales coaching? And why would in-depth knowledge of nitrogen flagship projects be relevant to business coaching? It's mind-boggling. I wonder how these people would react if they had appendicitis and the doctor told them: 'Oh, you're an engineer?

You should have told me. I'm afraid I can only perform appendix operations on florists.' I think they'd be somewhat confused. Or, a physiotherapist might shake his head and proclaim: 'Auditor? Out of the question. I've only ever given massages to bus drivers. They sit quite differently, you know.'

Sector-specific knowledge – very important in the world of business consulting. Consultants obviously need to know how a business functions, how its client's processes and structures are organized, where the sticking points are. Coaches are brought on board for a completely different reason: to enhance clear communication, awareness, self-leadership and confidence – and anyone can benefit, whether the person is a racing driver or the prime minister. Yes, fortunately! Ever since I had that conversation with the hand surgeon, these two little words bring a smile to my face. Let's see . . .

'But, you do know how an agency works? Otherwise you can't coach us, can you?'

'Yes, fortunately! Coaching works independently of how well I know the ins and outs of a particular business.' Smile . . . and done.

'But, can you really cure my fear of flying, so it'll never return?'

'Yes, fortunately!' A charming smile. That's settled, then.

This little combination of words is always a winner. Go on, try me!

But you know how it is when you're all set up to take on the world and suddenly you don't need to any more. An interesting phenomenon – you might be familiar with it. Since carrying my little magic formula like a Colt around my waist, ready to shoot, no one challenges me to a duel – or rather, no one questions my competence. Clients experience this phenomenon as well, by the way. After I've coached them to be prepared for even the most unlikely questions or challenges, everything suddenly runs smoothly – no awkward retorts, no grumbling, not a spanner in the works. Dealing with worst-case scenarios seems to facilitate best-case results. 'Right, that's how we'll do it' is the response my client gets in a meeting he had assured me would be 'a total bloody catastrophe'. In this particular case, it turned out, the worst-case scenario we'd prepared for happened only once in all the years since that session. Clarity begets clarity – ironclad law.

The other day . . . A make-up artist is wagging her hair curler dangerously close to my ear. 'So, the film director asked me if I can make scars and burns invisible. Pardon me?! How about reading my CV!' She's still upset. Most people get annoyed if someone questions their capabilities. Classic trigger point, with a domino effect: you get angry, justify yourself, sound tense and go colour-blind – there's only black and white, nothing in between. My advice to her: 'The next time a director asks if you can touch up burns, just say: "Yes, fortunately."' And, fortunately, she stops wagging the hair curler near my face and gives me a big smile. It has the same instant calming effect it had on me. End of drama.

If somebody questions your skills or capabilities, the key response is: don't take it personally. This attitude is so fundamental that I've devoted a whole chapter to it, a few pages further on – sentence 42: 'I won't take it personally.'

Let me just say that in the majority of cases a sceptic's questions reveal more about him or her than about the person whose abilities he or she has doubts about – another good reason not to take anything personally. Scepticism is simply an expression of concern, fear and doubt; at the very least, it's lacking in optimism. When, for example, a graphic designer is worried about missing a deadline, or a project leader fears she may have given the wrong person the job, then this agitation inevitably gives rise to questions. When people fear being seen as incompetent, they ask lots of questions to cover their backs. It's understandable; they want to feel certain. But it rarely works. Because, where a feeling is absent – in this instance, a feeling of certainty – logical arguments or an impressive track record won't assuage their doubts. They're far more likely to succeed if they react to a feeling with a feeling. Fear asks: 'Can you do it really, really well?' And confidence answers: 'Yes, fortunately!' A confidence-building measure that instantly works.

My advice is: it's always better not to feel insulted if someone questions your abilities – they have every right to. And it's our right to stay cool, calm and collected. See those situations as an invitation to practise self-assurance and confidence. And if someone really does insult you, this phrase might be useful: 'An insult is basically just a desperate cry for help.' A therapist once said this to me, and it makes perfect sense. It means: this person is unable to act differently at the moment; they need to make someone look small, in the vague hope that it will make them look bigger. And, of course, it never works, it just increases the anguish. Best to just brush it off and wish that person a 'speedy recovery' (see sentence 12).

So, if somebody ever asks you if you really are good at your job, think of that wonderful hand surgeon, relax, smile and give them a sprightly: 'Yes, fortunately!'

WHAT THIS SENTENCE GIVES YOU

TOLERANCE
CALMNESS
LIGHTNESS

38

I'D PREFER TO KEEP IT PROFESSIONAL

Leyla has been promoted. She's now the head of corporate communications, a fantastic job where she's responsible for all the areas she enjoys working in: press office, presentations, pitches, social media, and internal communication as well, of course – everything from e-books to podcasts. Fourteen wonderful people now work for her. And Leyla is in her early thirties – pretty impressive. She's got lots of ideas and loads of talent. What she doesn't have is a clear conscience. That's my first impression as I sit across from her on the roof of a multistorey car park which is now a hip beach club. It feels totally surreal to be hovering in this bright beach-vibe world, surrounded by skyscrapers.

'You sound as if you need to apologize for getting ahead so quickly,' I say to her, after she's told me about her promotion.

She nods, relieved. 'Yes, I feel guilty.'

'But, if you walk around with a T-shirt that says "I'm Sorry I'm the Boss", you're going to have a hard time.'

Leyla sighs, while her eyes follow two plastic flamingos gently drifting in the small swimming pool.

She explains that two of her favourite colleagues had applied for the job, but she hadn't. It was only when management explicitly suggested her that she became a competitor. Now she feels as if she's won a race she hadn't really entered, for which the others had trained for months. Leyla also faces another challenge: yesterday's buddies are today's subordinates (an old-fashioned term, I know, but it best describes the psychological dynamics involved here). She'll need to deal with that, and so will her team.

Hierarchical changes feel weird when we doubt ourselves while we're on the way up – and others will then automatically do the same. So, conflicts loom for Leyla and her team, as her clash with Dirk exemplifies.

They've worked together successfully on dozens of projects and always got on fabulously. But the other day, Dirk snapped at his new boss, over a minor issue: 'So, just do it yourself, since you can do everything better!' Leyla tells me, 'He'd never have dared do that with the previous head.' She's still so shocked that she meekly admits that she hasn't yet responded to the outburst. She'll have to clarify matters with Dirk, and that's precisely what we prepare for.

Three days later, a much more relaxed-sounding Leyla leaves a voicemail. After some initial nervousness, she'd plucked up her courage and taken the lead: 'My impression is, you feel there's a personal stake in this issue. Is this really about the topic at hand? And, if it is, could we please discuss it in a businesslike way, because your tone seems inappropriate to me. I'd prefer to keep it professional.' Dirk was silent for a bit – always a good sign.

'I'd prefer to keep it professional.' A relaxed, easy sentence with which to get your employees back on board, even when they'd rather splash around in the water. Here's something a client experienced just the other day. His legal division (of all people) advised him to turn a blind eye concerning a contract. The thing was that it was illegal, and he would have been liable. So, he said: 'I'd prefer to keep it professional.' How could they respond? 'But *we* don't!'?

Of course, you can rephrase the sentence. 'Let's have this conversation on a more professional level – I think that would make more sense,' for instance, or 'It's getting too personal for my liking. How about dealing with this on a professional level?' Depending on what best suits the situation.

Why do I use the term 'professional' here all the time? It takes us back to the subject of the inner child. I briefly discussed this under sentence 33: arguments, agitation and dramas often result from the fact that the easily excitable childish elements of our psyche have taken control. When that happens, nothing works on a professional level because that's not an ability a child has.

'You should have been there, Ms Kuschik, it was like a kindergarten!' is a lament I've often heard. 'Behaviour like *that* from the supervisory board! You can't imagine.' Actually, I can. And it's always the same story, which is why I usually answer: 'It *is* a kindergarten. Your boss sounds like a five-year-old, the CFO is like a rebellious teenager, and you were probably around eight years old – does that sound about right?' So far, everyone has either nodded, sighed or laughed when I put it like this. Because it's true. If someone presses our individual emotional trigger points, most of us cease to be grown-ups. We explode, and we certainly don't act like professionals. That's why 'I'd prefer to keep it professional' is like a nice little invitation to cut short the children's birthday party. A well-intentioned reminder that we're all adults and know better. Usually, this works pretty well. After all, self-leadership and assurance are best learnt when we're dealing with their opposites.

'I'm really fed up with having to spell everything out, it's unbelievable! Why doesn't anyone use their bloody brain!' The owner of the event agency is furious with his team. 'I'm forced to repeat everything a thousand times. I'm not going to say a single word from now on.' Sounds pretty petulant, I tell him, and he answers that he has every right to be. Which is true. I can generally empathize when it comes to that checkmate feeling. But this attitude won't bring about a solution.

'Jürgen Klopp must have felt like that, now and then,' I comment, and he gives me a look of incomprehension. 'There must have been many times he shouted the same thing again and again from the sideline, and no one took any notice. Yet, I expect he never asked himself whether he'd go and motivate his team at half-time, or just stay put and sulk. He's got to lead his team, no matter what – that's his job.' The agency boss gives me a sullen look. So much for football metaphors. I press on, regardless: 'So, Joachim Löw rushes into the dressing room and fumes: "You've really pissed me off! Right, I'm not saying a single word from now on – figure it out yourselves!"' At this point, he did at least give me a crooked smile.

It's just the way it is: if we allow our professional judgement to be tinged by personal sensibilities, we make life unnecessarily difficult for ourselves and others. It's more effective to stay professional, even if we're angry, someone is stealing our time, or we have a guilty conscience.

Do you know the story about the two monks by the river? I think it fits quite neatly here. During a long journey back to their monastery, a young and an elderly monk happen upon a river. An old woman is standing there, wishing to cross to the other shore, but she can't swim. There's no bridge or boat in sight. Although monks are forbidden to have bodily contact with a woman, the older monk tells her to climb on his back, and then swims her to the other side. After setting her down, the woman bows her head, respectfully, her palms pressed together. After the monk has returned to his companion, they continue their journey. The older monk's saffron-red habit has almost dried when the younger monk can no longer restrain himself. 'We're forbidden to even touch a woman!' he complains. 'Why did you do that?' The elderly monk listens patiently before answering: 'I brought the woman to the other side and left her there. You're still carrying her around with you.'

The thing about feeling guilty: it creates stress, and it's utterly superfluous. The person who created it needs a good talking to. And that's always and exclusively: us. Personal emotions can be a real hindrance to vocational progress. They don't get us anywhere, and they make us look small. These feelings can be stubborn. We think we've left them behind, watched them disappear in our rearview mirror, and suddenly they're right in front of us again. It's reassuring to have a sentence for them in our arsenal. 'I'd prefer to keep it professional' is a sentence Leyla still uses occasionally. In the meantime, she's been promoted to a position on the leadership team.

WHAT THIS SENTENCE GIVES YOU

CLARITY
ORIENTATION
RESPECT

39

I LOST TRACK OF TIME

I'm in my mid-twenties, attending a seminar for personal development in London, and it's pretty gruelling. For those of us with a truly open mind, it turns out to be a momentous experience – a masterclass in self-responsibility and integrity. It's a round-the-clock drill. I'm even thinking about the course while I'm lying in the bath in my hotel room in the evening. The person holding the seminar – a beautiful, wiry woman from LA – is particularly keen on giving us homework. An example: at the end of the first day, everyone in the group is asked to commit themselves to certain rules, until the following day. Punctuality is one of them: *9 a.m., sharp* is the deadline we have solemnly sworn to be back in our seats by.

As it turns out, not everyone takes their vows seriously. Roughly every tenth participant arrives late the next morning. Lady LA asks one of the latecomers – a stylishly dressed French dude who looks like a young Alain Delon – what took him so long. Elaborately, smiling all the while, he explains that he missed the tube by a hair's breadth. 'And what's the honest answer?' our coach asks, fixing him with a firm gaze.

'Excuse me?' Alain Delon is no longer smiling.

'What really happened?' she asks. 'And I only want to hear about *your* part in it. I'm sure the train wasn't there too early.'

Suddenly, the atmosphere in the room feels charged. We become witnesses to a riveting verbal obstacle race. Twenty minutes later the Frenchman's explanation goes like this: 'I missed the tube because I was late leaving the house. I was late leaving because I changed my clothes five times. I wanted to look good, but I couldn't decide what to wear. It's important to me to look good because I feel insecure.'

'All right. So, your vanity was more important to you than keeping your word and arriving here on time.'

The French guy swallows; Lady LA angles her head, expectantly. We're waiting. 'Alors . . . maybe, my *insecurity* was more important?'

They gaze at each other. Then she says, softly: 'OK, my dear, I'll accept that. It's always better when one says it one-self.' She laughs, disarmingly. Alain Delon looks relieved and we all start breathing normally again. Spontaneous clapping.

'I was too late because I feel insecure.' Sounds a little different from 'I missed the tube.' You can change your-self, but you can't change the London Underground. On the surface, this was merely a voyeuristic journey into the realm of vanity. Yet, the exercise demonstrates how we can delve into what really is by proceeding from one level to the next. This is also known as the onion-peeling method. 'Responsibility, folks!' is what the woman from LA keeps hollering, and responsibility is what this is all about. Punctuality is generally a great topic to apply it to: the last thing you want to hear when you're giving a seminar, and you have to keep repeating things for latecomers, are their excuses, which then take up even more time. And even our tolerance as a group begins to wane, as we become adept at detecting obvious attempts to shift blame on to circumstances. It's wonderful to see how everyone *de*-velops, in the true sense of the word (originally from the old French *développer*, meaning to unroll or unfold). I'm thinking to myself, 'When you spend three days fully focused on responsibility and excuses you become a good detective,' but then I'm jolted back into the proceedings as the coach vehemently dismisses another tale: 'Most of the others here made it on time. In the same city, with the same traffic. Don't believe your own bullshit.' 'Yes ma'am!' I'm thinking, as I imagine myself breathlessly jogging through Paddington station the next morning, balancing a cup of Earl Grey.

So, this seminar in London really impressed me, and to this day I'd rather someone who's kept me waiting says 'Sorry, I'm not with it this morning' than 'I couldn't find a parking space'. Why not be honest? 'I completely underestimated the time it takes to find a parking space,' I heard someone panting the other day as he was rushing towards a neighbouring table in a restaurant. That impressed me. Or, as this chapter is headed: 'I lost track of time.'

Perhaps you're now thinking: 'What does it matter how someone says it?' If so, I disagree. Experience shows that taking responsibility is far more readily accepted by someone kept waiting than a story packed full of justifications. I've personally experienced this a hundred times. And even most latecomers will eventually agree. 'It was such a relief to just say it straight out,' a film director told me recently. After a lot of doubts, he'd managed to persuade himself to adopt a new strategy. As an experiment, so to speak. He was surprised, and correspondingly pleased, with how easy it was to just quickly admit: I forgot, I messed up, I lost track. Much simpler than concocting the usual brew of white lies and evasions.

And there it is again, the positive effect of the negative I-message – we touched on the subject before. If you can be crystal clear and say, 'This is all my fault. I completely forgot about our meeting,' you'll immediately soothe your guilty conscience. Boldly, and as a matter of course, taking responsibility for your fallibility always has a calming effect. Like sentences 10 ('I don't know') and 26 ('I made a mistake'), 'I lost track of time' has a powerful pacifying effect. Because, once you've admitted to your part in creating a situation, who's going to demand you do so again? What would be the point?

'I lost track of time', a sentence that will make your life easier, is really just a placeholder for any statement expressing a responsible excuse. I chose it because it fits so well into our fast-paced lives. Chances are you'll have plenty of opportunities to use it – like, the next time you have back-to-back meetings, or when you realize that there's just no way you're going to be sitting on your seat at nine o'clock in the morning.

'If you really want something, you'll find a way. If you don't, you'll find an excuse', as the saying goes – and if someone hadn't already invented it, I'd be happy if it was me. Because it also contains the message: if you want something, you take responsibility for it. Determined, clear, active. If, on the other hand, you're always ducking out of things, you automatically end up in the murky valley of justifications where blame doesn't exist because there are always excuses. Or, as a sales manager once flippantly remarked: 'If someone can't swim, it's always because they're wearing the wrong bathing trunks.'

The next time you start out late, lose track of time or forget an appointment, just say it clearly and take responsibility. Honestly admitting 'I lost track of time' is more of a relief than you might think. The sentence is true, shows you have class, and is always appreciated.

WHAT THIS SENTENCE GIVES YOU
SELF-DETERMINATION
FREEDOM
HONESTY

I LOST TRACK OF TIME

It's quite astounding how uneasy many of us feel when it comes to compliments, and the different emotions positive feedback can trigger in us – provided we get it. This is certainly the case in my home country, Germany. Under sentence 7 I called it 'a praise-starved country', and I'm pretty sure it's not the only one. And it's true, isn't it? Praise, admiration, paying compliments is not generally a priority in interpersonal relationships. So, it's only logical that many find it hard to casually accept a compliment – we simply haven't practised it. And that, in turn, makes the payer of a compliment wonder whether they should do so again. It's a vicious circle. But while sentence 7 – 'This is what I truly admire about you' – was about reluctance to pay compliments, sentence 40 is about the exact opposite: the ability to feel completely at ease when you receive one.

'That's a beautiful dress. You look fantastic in it!' – 'You reckon? It's really old.'

'That's a lovely coat!' – 'Really? It hardly cost anything.' Oh well, then.

'What a lovely bag!' – 'Seriously? I thought of throwing it away the other day.'

Typical reactions to compliments concerning how we look, our taste, our style. Incredulity, followed by depreciation based on cheapness or age. I doubt anyone paying a compliment wants to hear that. And looking at these exchanges, the only thing I find incredible is the incredulity about receiving a compliment. Honestly, what does this say about us? Do we want to send the message that we bought the ugliest item we could find? Of course we like the things we own – that's why we wanted to have them. That's why we wear them. That's why we paid for them. Why is simply saying 'Thank you!' so difficult?

When I'm coaching, the answer to this question is often along the lines of 'I don't want to come across as though I'm bragging' or 'I'm not someone who defines himself by what he owns – I prefer to be modest' or 'I don't like to be the centre of attention'. I get all that, but it has little to do with a willingness to accept compliments. I think this is where people get confused. It's not about spending half an hour basking in the glittering radiance of a compliment, before stepping up to the Olympic winner's podium to collect your medal. It's more to do with the basics of having pleasant everyday interactions. Accept out of sheer politeness, if nothing else. 'That's a lovely coat!' 'Oh, thanks!' Or even with a dash of self-confidence: 'Isn't it? I love this coat.'

It gets even harder, for a lot of people, when the compliment pertains to their expertise, know-how, or a talent. Who's going to respond with 'Yes, I'm really good at this, thank you', or 'I like that about myself too'? Not many, I'd say. I'd like to propose it as an option all the same. You might be surprised how easily it's said, and how big a favour you're doing the person who has paid the compliment. Ideally, both parties benefit from a present. Those receiving it are happy, and that joy reflects generously on the presenter – a wonderful mirror effect.

For decades, a very successful and generally open-minded former client of mine – let's call her Simone – would never consider the option of thanking someone for a compliment. When she received one, she'd clam up, couldn't handle it. At the same time, she's astoundingly capable, has a high degree of emotional intelligence, and is admired by her roughly 400 employees and by the members of the management board. Yet, because she never learnt to accept compliments graciously, she began to be seen in a different light. 'Insecure, cold, indecisive' is how people started to perceive her, she told me in our initial briefing session. No one, least of all Simone, had any real idea what brought about this change in people's perception.

The good thing about an impression is that it doesn't necessarily have anything to do with the truth, with who you really are. It doesn't describe a person; it describes what certain behaviours trigger in us. In other words, it's merely an interpretation of someone's actions or demeanour because we don't have a better explanation for them. That's why a coach is often like a tracker, looking for traces, to find out what is really going on.

Simone isn't making it easy for me. In our very first session she tells me how important modesty is to her. 'We don't make others go out of their way for us' was the mantra of her childhood. 'If someone offers you something, say "No, thank you,"' her parents taught her. 'We don't want people to have to lug bottles of lemonade up from the cellar just for us and, later, have to clean the glasses.' Downplaying compliments was a part of this etiquette. The kids shouldn't get big-headed when they achieved something – others will think you're arrogant! Two very clear messages: don't cause trouble, don't flatter yourself! Heard it so often, complied so many times, that these doctrines were etched on to Simone's mind decades ago. So, there's a little policeman inside her who says: 'The law of good manners requires you to never accept anything, and never try to impress others!' It's hardly surprising, then, that forty years on, in a responsible position, she still hates compliments, clams up, looks away and mumbles something like: 'No, no, it was a team effort.' That's what the doctrine, the little truncheon-waving policeman in her head, demands. Appealing to logic doesn't get me anywhere with Simone, and my feeling advises that a provocative approach is more likely to succeed.

'In a way, it's quite rude of you.'

'What? Me? Rude? The opposite, I'd say!'

I won't be deterred. 'Not for your host. You're attacking him on two fronts.'

'Is this a joke?!' A person who has suppressed her own feelings and desires all her life is bound to be horrified by this accusation – the gall!

Later, after I've told her what reactions her behaviour might provoke, she starts to give it some thought. For example, people who love to entertain and be the host feel as if the rug's been pulled from under their feet. And there are those who definitely do feel bothered when a guest makes them feel like they shouldn't have bothered. Simone never saw it from that angle before. She never considered that there are people who really would like to bake a cake for her, or who love to be able to offer their guests a choice of three different types of milk; that her attitude deprived others of their joy in giving simply never occurred to her. And so, it is possible for such age-old mental constructs – based, in this instance, on inappropriate modesty and politeness – to begin to crumble. Applied to praise, this means: someone pays us a compliment ('Here you are!'), and another person receives it ('Thank you!'). Exactly – we're already practised at doing precisely that. Oddly, though, it seems to be more difficult when it comes to happily acknowledging a compliment.

To recap, people who can't accept compliments are depriving others of joy; they come across as insecure and somehow exude an aura of subtle hostility. Imagine a birthday party. You arrive with your beautifully wrapped present and the person whose birthday it is says: 'You needn't have! Put it over there – you can take it with you when you leave.' There'd be a few raised eyebrows, at least. But, let's be clear: that's exactly the situation when we can't accept a compliment. The other person feels dispensable, or even rejected. And it doesn't exactly make you, the receiver of the compliment, feel good either.

Looking at it in this way helped Simone overcome the difficulties she was facing surprisingly quickly. Since redefining her concept of politeness, things are running smoothly at work and she comes across as a self-assured and confident leadership personality. So, the next time someone says 'You're looking really good, energized!' you might like to think of Simone, and just say: 'Wow, that's nice! Thanks for the compliment!'

WHAT THIS SENTENCE GIVES YOU

SELF-RESPECT

JOY

GRATITUDE

Esther is the most enthusiastic person I've ever met. She first appeared in my life, along with a seemingly endless supply of positive energy, when I was working as a broadcasting assistant for a German station called RIAS TV. She's twenty-two, I'm two years older, and the broadcaster is now called Deutsche Welle TV (DW for short, a kind of German version of the BBC World Service). 'You look like a nice person!' she says, beaming at me. 'We haven't met yet. I'm Esther from DW's Spanish service!' Open, cheerful, kind. Socializing certainly isn't her weak point. I quickly find out that she's studying Romance linguistics, her star sign is Aquarius, and she's just returned from teaching a two-week intensive Spanish course for young people in Majorca. The ratio of students to teachers was unfavourable this time, she tells me: too few students, 'so the head told us, just before the course got started, that some classes would be given by two teachers in tandem. Of course, I immediately objected,' she happily jabbers on. 'That's out of the question, for me.'

'Ah. OK. And why is that?' I ask, genuinely curious.

'Well, I told them it just wouldn't work for me. I'm much too dominant for that!'

'I'm much too dominant for that'?! Wow, quite a statement, very self-assured. I'm impressed, and also astonished when she tells me what the reaction was. 'They immediately accepted it,' says Esther. 'I mean, it would have been pointless otherwise.' Right, obviously. I'm wondering how she manages to sound so matter-of-fact about it, as if she'd said: 'Can't drink that: I'm lactose intolerant.' 'Ah, glad you mentioned it. No dairy milk for you, then. The oat milk's right over there.' Not so difficult, perhaps. But when the topic is dominance? I thought back then, and I still do, that the key to this is clarity. Here, clearly, the law of attraction comes into play. Esther feels so at ease with this aspect of her character that she's able to talk about it quite naturally, which in turn reduces the likelihood that others will be judgemental about it. It's especially impressive when someone can nonchalantly mention a quirk that would generally be considered a flaw. That's a sign of real class.

I remember a client who, after we'd had five sessions together, suddenly heard himself quite casually say, in a meeting, 'No, I'd better not do that. I'm much too insecure for that.'

'What?! You, insecure? I'd say you were extremely self-confident.'

'True, and part of that is self-*awareness*. And I'm aware enough to know that I'd feel insecure.'

That sentence, that exchange, had a liberating effect on him, and the others also learnt something – albeit they were a bit astonished. The lesson here is that seemingly contradictory character traits don't automatically cancel each other out, even if that might, at first, sound paradoxical. Contradictory traits can in fact exist quite happily alongside each other. We can be clear *and* warm-hearted, empathic *and* intolerant. These traits, for instance, aren't incompatible.

'I'm much too intolerant for that!' I once told a friend whose astonished response was: 'Whaaat?! You, who always understands EVERYONE?!' Yes. I have understanding for almost everyone and everything. Yet this doesn't mean that I don't have an attitude to things. I understand people *and* I don't always like what I'm understanding. Being empathic doesn't necessarily mean I share another person's way of thinking. In fact, empathy *and* intolerance can go quite well together.

Here's an example. For decades I couldn't stand it when people around me sniffed (as in clearing your nose of mucus). It was as if someone flipped a switch and my tolerance level instantly dropped to zero. To my ears, sniffing was an unacceptable noise-harassment. Full stop. I tried everything when it came to this unsavoury social phenomenon: dispensing paper hankies, hypnotherapy, endless discussions, humour, coaching, rhetorical strokes of genius. If you can think of anything else, I probably did that too. Fact is, I didn't want to tolerate it, and I'll only ever capitulate when there's simply no choice. On a Chinese subway train, perhaps, or at the Holy Festival in Mumbai. It's always good to know when you're beaten. Yet it wasn't there, or in a crowded market somewhere in Asia, that I finally managed to resolve this annoying issue. Rather, it was during a short train journey between Düsseldorf and Cologne.

It's a December day – flu season. The carriage is full of wheezing and coughing people. In fact, it's more like an ear, nose and throat specialist's waiting room – my idea of hell. I've got a window seat and I've, cheekily, blocked the seat next to me with my bag. But at the main station in Düsseldorf a man, plainly exhausted, plonks himself down next to me. I only just manage to pull the bag, containing my laptop, away. That's when I hear the first sniff – though that word's inadequate; the noise this man's producing sounds more like someone using a straw to suck up the remains of a milkshake. Instantly, I'm no longer in Düsseldorf's main station but in Intolerance Central. My heart clams up and my brain seeks retribution. Before I'm able to consider a measured response, I can hear myself saying, clearly and a bit too loudly: 'This isn't going to work.'

'Uh . . . are you talking to me?' he asks, taken aback.

'Yes, I mean you. You and me: this isn't going to work. You are sitting next to the country's most intolerant person when it comes to sniffing.'

'I've got a cold!' he croaks, sounding peeved and puzzled in equal measure.

'I realize that,' I say. 'When I have a cold, I use a hand-kerchief.' I'm talking as if I'd been given a truth serum – not exactly charming. But then, neither is his straw-milkshake abomination.

He's flabbergasted. 'So, you'd prefer it if I blew my nose the whole time?'

'Exactly.' That's all I say, and he seems lost for words too.

We stare at each other, and I'm beginning to feel guilty. I can tell he's obviously struggling with himself. Then he suddenly turns to me again and says, almost ceremoniously, 'I will try not to do it.'

I'm touched. I reply: 'And I will try to ignore it.'

And then we both start laughing.

The train arrives in Cologne, and he hasn't sniffed once. A bit of a shame, I'm thinking: I would have liked to have had the opportunity to be tolerant.

What can I say? This chance meeting on the train had a curative effect. Sniffing is no longer an issue. I wonder whether the man still remembers the incident, after all these years. Anyway, here's my belated 'thank you'. How wonderful if you, the unknown Mr Sniff, happen to be reading these words right now. I always wanted to express my admiration: what you did took guts!

'I'm much too dominant / insecure / intolerant / self-aware / shy / egotistical for that.' Any one of these is a startlingly honest sentence, an expression of self-reflection that undoubtedly benefits the person who says it as well as the person hearing it. It's always good to know who you are dealing with, and, by the same token, the least we can do is get to know ourselves – after all, this is the longest relationship we'll have in our lives.

So, best not wait too long. Get to know yourself as soon as possible and as thoroughly as possible. Acquaint yourself with your qualities, dislikes and doubts, dispassionately, just taking note of them. As I've mentioned in a previous chapter, the principle here is STOP (State The Obvious Promptly). This little habit can be enormously useful. It lets others know who they are dealing with, and gives you a better understanding of yourself. To deny who you are is pointless anyway. Most people try to do this at some point, but it never works. Inauthenticity is always detected.

Much better to be self-assured and confident. 'I'm much too —— for that' is a step in this direction. Simply stating what is can be extremely liberating. Show people who you really are, the full size of yourself. Rest assured, it won't hurt anyone.

WHAT THIS SENTENCE GIVES YOU

CALMNESS
SELF-ASSUREDNESS
INNER PEACE

42

I WON'T TAKE IT PERSONALLY

Kara Johnstad is a fantastic singer, a truly self-determined woman who enjoys accomplishing her goals and helping others to accomplish theirs. When she isn't giving a concert or running her School of Voice, she likes to skip barefoot through the semi-circular practice room she calls her 'Oval Office', singing and pausing only to sit at her Steinway grand piano on which she accompanies her students when they're singing. She's always warm-hearted, always positive. I used to attend her school quite regularly. I love singing.

I remember one lesson in December – or rather, the bit after the lesson, as I was preparing to leave. I'm in the hallway, putting my winter gear on and bracing myself for the trek through the Berlin snow, when Anne comes in. Her lesson is next. 'Can you hear that?' She's in a huff.

I'm fidgeting with my fringe under my hood, looking at her in the wardrobe mirror. 'What?'

'She's singing again!' Anne complains, pulling her scarf from her neck. 'I could hear it all the way downstairs, as I was coming in!'

'Well, she is . . .' I say, hesitating to state the obvious, 'a singer?' I'm not sure what she's getting at, so I turn round and face her.

'She knows bloody well that I find it hard to loosen up when I'm singing. She's doing that on purpose, to spite me!'

'Ah. Who would have guessed?' I'm thinking as I grab my gloves, relieved to be going. It must be very strenuous always to take things personally.

Projection is the term psychoanalysts use to describe this phenomenon. Not a typical life-coaching topic, incidentally, but a common issue in the business world, because not everyone who has climbed the career ladder has also moved up on a personal level. If you lack self-awareness – in the literal sense of not being aware of who you are – you're going to feel insecure, or even inferior, as a person; you'll tend to doubt yourself and easily take things personally. People who've been stuck in this rut know: it's easy to feel hurt, to view neutral statements as attacks, and even to misinterpret well-intentioned comments as negative feedback. That can be pretty tiring – for others, too, because all these interpretations, accusations and justifications can turn the world around you into a veritable minefield.

That someone lacks assurance isn't always instantly apparent, and this adds to the difficulties. If someone feels inferior, they often come across as arrogant, easily provoked or cynical. In other cases, they may seem to be trying to ingratiate themselves. There are many ways to camouflage a complex.

'I won't take it personally' is therefore my sentence for

everyone who is familiar with this issue. The other person probably isn't even acting *against* you, but simply *for* themselves – that, too, can be a very rewarding insight, providing an exit strategy from a drama. I dealt with this in a different context under sentence 2 ('This isn't against you, it's for me').

If you're someone who tends to take things personally, simply resolving not to want to do so any more can already make a real difference. Since our feelings are determined by our thoughts, a new, positive thought will automatically produce a new and better feeling. 'I won't take it personally' is one of these new thoughts, or thought-sentences if you prefer. It sounds simultaneously determined and light – which is always a good place to start.

It's also a good idea for people who easily feel attacked to take the trouble to question the motivation of the person who is 'attacking' them, rather than instantly being offended. Why is he or she acting like this? What other reasons could there be to do or say something? Questions which enable us to consider alternatives and broaden our horizon, rather than simply creating alleged truths out of uncertainty.

'What other people think of you isn't really any of your business,' I once told a client. He was taken aback. Yet, after recovering from the shock, he found this perspective quite comforting. We both had to laugh. It sounds provocative, I know, but I intentionally formulated it in such a pointed manner because it's so true. To say it as an affirmation, all we need to do is take the sting out of it. Then it sounds like this: 'People can think whatever they want.' It often helps people to have these comforting sentences at the back of their minds, so they can say them to themselves in stressful situations, as a quiet mantra. And it's the way it is: people do think whatever they want, whether we like it or not. Sometimes, nothing we can say or do will change what someone thinks, and the sooner we accept this, the sooner our lives become easier.

Of course, it also happens that someone – like Anne – feels so threatened that they mount an all-out offensive. Have you ever been the target? 'You're doing it on purpose! Admit it!' That's usually quite a startling experience, especially when it's not true. But, you know how to deal with it: just select one of the many de-escalation tools you now have at your disposal – a good way to quickly clarify matters.

If the other person then still obstinately claims that you mounted a premeditated attack, I suggest Plan Easy. In my world, that means letting go. Just let go. Because, if someone insists on being angry they obviously need to have this experience, at this point. Let the other person do their thing, and remember: you're not responsible for the experiences others wish to have. Inside, everyone is in their own world as they move about this planet. Who can say what issue someone is really trying to address at a particular moment?

If you can honestly say that your intentions were good, yet someone else desperately wants to interpret them as a hostile act, so be it. Whether you tend more towards Anne or Kara, the real question is never 'How did the *other* person mean that?' but rather 'How do *you* wish to take it?' This question gives us the freedom to react in a way that is best for us, at any particular time. 'I won't take it personally' is always the better choice.

WHAT THIS SENTENCE GIVES YOU

FREEDOM
CLARITY
SELF-AWARENESS

43

I PREFER TALKING *WITH* PEOPLE TO TALKING *ABOUT* THEM

reezing cold in the middle of summer. I'm sitting in one of those ghastly designed conference rooms where people are at the mercy of technology. The windows can't be opened, the blinds – triggered by the sun – keep rolling up and down, and even their slats are adjusted automatically so that the atmosphere created by the light keeps changing every few minutes. The air-conditioning wafts frigid air around us, and even the maintenance technician has to concede that he can't change this, after his third attempt to alter its settings has failed. At least the cold is in line with the mood, as I see when I look at the expressions on the nine attendees who face each other across the table wearing jackets and scarves in the middle of July.

Crisis meeting in Baden-Baden. The reason for it: rumours have been ripping like wildfire through the marketing department, and my client is the head of this team. He's convened this little summit, and I've been asked to moderate it, as a mediator – a job I'll only accept if there's a real emergency. I mean, why would anyone voluntarily place themselves between two warring factions? But, since my client doesn't think he can do the job, already has three disciplinary warning letters on his desk and the issue has become really urgent and needs to be resolved, I've made an exception.

So, what's happened? For weeks now, most of those gathered here have been complaining about each other and spreading rumours. Accusations, justifications, denunciations, defensiveness, anger and frustration all around. There are nicer reasons to hold a meeting, but it turns out that my job is relatively easy because everyone is displaying precisely the behaviour they're accusing their colleagues of. *What bothers me*, I write on the whiteboard, and then I list everything the team members bellow at me: bad-mouthing others, denouncing team members to those higher up, spreading rumours as if they were certainties – those are the top three complaints. Therefore, what's missing here is integrity. And the question is, how are they going to transform this insight into positive action?

How about 'We don't talk *about* people, we talk *with* them?', I suggest after no one offers any ideas. Spontaneous agreement all around. Everyone finds this proposal reasonable and says they'll keep to it. One reason being, I should think, that it's also a good way to protect yourself. The sentence I wrote becomes the starting point for a lively discussion that can be described as committed and even playful, at times. In the end it almost becomes a little melodramatic as each team member stands up in solidarity to demonstrate acceptance of the new rules. A new beginning for the department – or at least a convincing declaration of intent.

A call to action can be a beautiful thing, especially when

you get to formulate it yourself. From now on, if some-one in the team wants to disparage someone else there's no need for the others to get nervous; their response is clear: 'We agreed to talk *with* people . . . Why don't you ask Ulrike directly what she meant? I think that would be the easiest solution.' Say it, turn round, get on with your job. It's a good formula for autonomy and for freeing yourself from entanglements pre-emptively, before things get out of hand.

'I prefer talking with people to talking about them' is a statement that immediately shows where you stand, and what you won't stand for. You can also say it in a more con-ciliatory way: 'As long as I don't know the whole story I'd rather not get involved', or 'I'd rather not comment, it's too much effort'. Sure, if someone is really intent on gossiping, or bad-mouthing someone else, you'll be seen as a spoil-sport. The person is likely to take your reaction personally. That's why the *way* it's said is important. The sentence headlining this chapter is an I-message and works like a mirror: people who are loyal to themselves and their feel-ings allow others to see themselves more clearly. Reactions like 'What's wrong with a bit of gossip?' or 'What's this moral finger-wagging, all of a sudden?' are simply a reflec-tion of the other person's guilty conscience.

I have always found it best to avoid getting involved in office gossip. Rumours never have a positive outcome. What's the advantage in bad-mouthing others? Has it ever resolved anything? Does it make the world a better place? Does it ever make the person we are talking badly about a better person? 'Oh, come on, gossiping is just having a bit of fun!' I'm not so sure; I've very rarely had that experience. Do we really feel lighter, more joyful or relieved when we've gossiped? When I *have* done so, I always felt a bit dirty afterwards.

On the other hand, a whole industry seems to do very well out of it. Just look at the gossip magazines. I sometimes have the feeling that many people know more rumours about celebrities than they know truths about themselves. I mentioned in another chapter that a therapist once told me that disparaging others is a cry for help. Makes sense to me. People who feed on gossip and bad-mouthing others probably aren't at ease with themselves.

There's a useful tool for this: THINK. An easy and effective acronym, a handy device to use and share with others. Each of the five letters stands for a smart little question – a simple checklist. Before you talk about someone else, ask yourself whether what you are about to say is really

T – true?
H – helpful?
I – inspiring?
N – necessary?
K – kind?

If not, it's better not to say it. It won't improve your situation. And I believe that's really what life is about: what can I do to improve the overall situation and to stay true to myself?

Incidentally, the marketing department in Baden-Baden is working harmoniously again. Two team members have left, three new people have joined. When the head of marketing conducted the job interviews, he asked each candidate what he or she thought of the statement 'I prefer talking with people to talking about them'. He'd had it framed and it hung in his office – which I thought was overdoing it a bit, but there you go. The three who got the job apparently found the statement particularly pertinent.

WHAT THIS SENTENCE GIVES YOU
A CLEAR CONSCIENCE
LOYALTY
GOOD KARMA

Dr Saarlander is a brilliant dermatologist – friendly, communicative, intelligent. And he has the most beautiful hands. With unerring confidence, he manages to find the root cause of ailments and often makes diagnoses his colleagues hadn't even considered. His patients respect and adore him for these qualities, and probably also for his colourful and tastefully designed private clinic. The waiting room looks more like the lounge of a boutique hotel than, well, a doctor's waiting room. Instead of the usual assortment of old magazines, thick high-quality coffee-table books are displayed on a low-slung velvet-draped sideboard; there's a discreet whiff of wellness in the air, like a perfume. If I had to give it a score from 1 (for stuffy) to 10 (for excellent) I'd give it 11.

No second chance for a first impression – this simple logic is beautifully manifested here. And this is precisely what the surgery's new internet portal is supposed to reflect, as Dr Saarlander tells me after one of the regular evening events that are held on the premises. Unfortunately, he's unhappy with the web design agency he's commissioned for the job. Although the team from the agency made an impressive pitch, none of the concepts have yet been realized. All Dr Saarlander has been offered so far is hot air – especially frustrating for someone so devoted to aesthetics.

'You're a brilliant wordsmith,' he compliments, 'so what do you tell people when you're confronted with sheer incompetence?'

'Hmm . . . cancel the contract?'

'And, assuming that isn't an option?' the man with the hands of a pianist responds while he looks around for somewhere to place his glass (and while I ask myself why it isn't an option).

'Giving my best only makes sense if you give your best, you said to me the other day – remember?' He nods. I really liked the sentence, and now I'm happy to repeat it back to him. 'If you combine it with a question, it might be a wake-up call for people who expect a lot and give nothing,' I tell him, in reference to the story he has just told me: that his team had immediately given the agency all the information they had requested, but they've heard nothing since. Three weeks have now passed. He sighed, clearly astounded by this blatant example of double standards.

'So, what's the question you would ask them?'

A few days later Dr Saarlander gets in touch to give me the good news. He finally managed to get the web designer on the phone and said to him: 'Giving my best only makes sense if you give your best. My question to you is therefore: is what I've experienced over the past few weeks really your best?' Those were his words to the web designer, no diplomatic faffing around before getting to the point. Always fascinating to see how someone will respond to a move like that. In this case all went well, as the doctor's no-nonsense approach cleared the way for a more committed, clearer form of communication. That's often the result when the question concerns self-assessment. 'Is this really your best?' prompts us to reflect before we get mired in justifications. It certainly had this effect on the web designer. He frankly admitted that his timing was catastrophic, that he had promised several clients the same deadline and didn't have the means to satisfy the intricate wishes of his clients – the agency, he conceded, had overestimated its capacities. Well, if that isn't a more favourable basis on which to negotiate . . .

But even if the man had barked back at him, the situation would have been improved. Let's imagine the worst-case scenario . . .

Dr Saarlander: 'Giving my best only makes sense if you give your best . . .'

Web Designer: 'Are you insinuating that we're not doing our job?'

Dr Saarlander: 'Insinuating? No. I'm describing the facts. You *haven't* been doing your job, for weeks. I wasn't even able to reach you. So, that's why I'm asking: is this your best? I mean it. Because if that's the case we'll obviously have to revoke our decision.'

So, whatever the reaction, the question is an invitation to clarify matters.

What I experience time and time again is that, no matter how badly someone treats us, many of us shy away from confrontation. We don't want to come across as bossy, or bring others into an awkward situation, and we desperately try to find a way of formulating our complaint so it'll sound diplomatic. The solution is: stop searching. Unpleasant truths don't become less so just because they're neatly packaged, with a bow tied around them.

Perhaps it is a consolation to know that it's not our job to shield others from the consequences of their actions. We all make decisions, and every decision has an effect. Why not allow our fellow humans to experience their own effects? We don't have to protect others from themselves. Otherwise, aren't we depriving them of the chance to learn?

'Giving my best only makes sense if you give your best' is a sentence that can be helpful in all sorts of situations, in the workplace as well as in our private lives, when interacting with employees, children, service providers or – like the other day – the lady in the bakery shop.

A small, chubby woman with beautiful red curls is bossing me around the shop: 'stand over there' / 'let the gentleman through' / 'careful your bag doesn't collide with the lids for the coffee'. Short little commands, barked at me from behind the counter while she has a private conversation with her colleague. Her hands are in motion, but they're not doing anything that would speed up the processing of my order. After I've repeated 'Two spelt currant buns, please' for the third time, I lose patience.

'Pardon me. Doing my best will only work, I think, if you do your best too.'

She glares at me. 'You what?!'

'Well, I've repeated myself three times, and now I'd like to be heard. You don't appear to be focused.'

'Because I'm not!' she shouts across the cream horns,

and then a little quieter, more to herself, 'What a day it's been!'

'Ah, I know those days too,' I say, to calm things again.

'That's all right, then,' she says, in a conciliatory tone. She's gazing at an empty display tray while her colleague is smiling at a male customer standing next to me. 'There . . . our last two spelt currant buns!' the colleague says, and the man pays for them. What can I say? That's what happens when two other people are doing their best, in parallel. The cream horns looked better anyway . . .

As you'll have noticed, the sentence isn't a softener, more a wake-up call which stirs things up a little. A reset, to get things back on track. Figuratively speaking: you lean out of the window with it, but not so far as to fall out. It's an appeal for higher standards, and it's never quite certain which direction the conversation will then take. In the case of the good doctor, it definitely moved things forward. The web designer accepted responsibility and personally saw to it that the job was done professionally. He could just as well have bailed out. Our little sentence only establishes clarity – it doesn't guarantee a happy ending. But clarity itself often makes us happier.

It is always the challenge that helps us to progress. If we stay in our comfort zone and never take risks we can't grow. Is it pleasant? No. Is it helpful? Yes. Especially if you're someone who thrives on harmony it's important occasionally to overcome your reluctance and make a con-frontational statement, because that's the best way to re-establish harmony. Sometimes it's best to take the bull by the horns.

So 'Giving my best only makes sense if you give your best' is an invitation for better collaboration, and is also a way to establish clarity through confrontation. The web design agency did finally ensure that my doctor friend's presence on the internet was appropriately stylish. Unfortunately for me, a few years later he went to live in Canada. So, if you happen to know a really good dermatologist . . .

WHAT THIS SENTENCE GIVES YOU

CERTAINTY
CLARITY
SELF-CONFIDENCE

45

I DON'T KNOW
HOW TO, SO
I'LL JUST
GIVE IT A GO

Asked, during a casting, whether he could ride a horse, the brilliant actor Sabin Tambrea answered: 'Yes, I can ride. I just have to learn to do it.' What a great sentence! He told this story on a popular German television chat show, NDR Talk Show, and the host was thrilled with the answer, which I can well understand, as it expresses an amazing attitude. Apparently Tambrea did finally get the role. I remember him, at any rate, riding on horseback in *Rübezahl – Lord of the Mountains* as Ludwig II of Bavaria, so the strategy seems to have been successful.

What appeals to me is the matter-of-factness of the statement. It was as if he wasn't bothered that he didn't have the ability at that precise moment; if you're keen to learn, you can do anything – at some point, at any rate. That's probably the secret of success: the willingness to constantly keep learning. One could also say that the word 'but' (as in, 'I'd love to but I can't ride') has rarely brought progress to the world, or prompted people to grow beyond their limitations.

*

And yet, it would be wrong to claim that the world belongs exclusively to the courageous and that only risk-takers get ahead. The world belongs to all of us. We can all walk, tie our shoes and open a carton of juice. We couldn't always do these things – we likely failed miserably at them at first, in fact. Then we had our breakthroughs, and after a while we never wasted another thought on shoelaces. Walking, cycling, driving, skiing, piano-playing, tap dancing, speaking Italian – the same principle applies: 'I don't know how to, so I'll just give it a go.' A wonderful sentence that turns mental barriers into opportunities. It takes us from can't do, via trying, to can do.

So many adults, with a mixture of determination and resignation, have tried to convince me during workshops that they're unable to do something and therefore will never learn it. 'I've never been able to do that!' they often protest, as if this were the clinching argument for never moving beyond where they are. Fact is, we were all unable to do anything once upon a time. Until we were able to do things. That's the essence of progress. And, isn't that the wonderful thing about being human? That we can constantly reinvent ourselves. There's something you can't do? Fantastic! Do it anyway. It's called *learning*.

Making big decisions always involves risks. To some, this may sound brash. Hasn't it got a lot to do with the type of person you are, your character? Not everyone's the same. This is true, of course. Nonetheless, in my experience, having worked with very different types of people, it has always been a good idea, for any person, to occasionally take a risk. Someone who is reticent will take a risk reticently. The introvert takes a gamble in an introverted sort of way, and the daring will of course be daring. But, surely, daring to take a risk is something we can all do, whatever our character. We did it all the time when we were kids. It's just a fact that doubts, fears and reservations don't get us anywhere, and they usually lead to procrastination – that well-known state where we're always putting things off.

Of course, I also sometimes have doubts. When I do, I find this wise little sentence useful: 'When in doubt, simply make your next step a little shorter.' I find that reassuring. And it still advocates progress rather than stagnation. Whether you run, stumble or crawl, you're moving forward. Most of us experience this in a positive way. We have a built-in motor and love to get ahead. That's why, in the evenings, when things calm down, when the day is done and sleep is almost upon us, it's usually the doubters who can't find peace. Because doubt nourishes our guilty conscience, and that switches on when we'd like to switch off: 'Perhaps I should . . . If only I had . . . What does he think of me now? . . . I'll just send an email . . . Wait a minute: I don't have to send a bloody email!' 'Mindfuck' is what Petra Bock calls this in her book of that title.

'I don't know how to, so I'll just give it a go' offers an easy way out of this maze. Don't ponder, just do it. Do it badly, perhaps. Maybe even fail. It's not that important. And if you do fail, just read sentence 9 again: 'I think I'd better forgive myself.' It's always better to be generous to yourself and to others. After all, we're not talking about the end of the world.

So, the next time you're hit by a big wave of wavering, that I-can't-do-it feeling, my advice is to do it anyway and then marvel at the result. Let's have a little more spirit of freedom, and perhaps even turn a lacklustre 'I suppose I could give it a try' into a joyful 'I don't know how to, so I'll just give it a go' – to truly miraculous effect.

WHAT THIS SENTENCE GIVES YOU
SELF-CONFIDENCE
COURAGE
PUTS A SMILE ON YOUR FACE

I DON'T KNOW HOW TO . . .

46

I DON'T WANT TO SUPPORT YOU IN YOUR WEAKNESS

Miriam is in tears. Over the weekend her husband told her he's fallen in love with another woman. He wants an immediate divorce and is moving out in two days' time. So, just like that, her whole life has come apart. A life both of them had created together: their house in Königstein, the company, the dog, two cats, their boat and the apartment on the island of Sylt. At least there are no children to worry about – Pit never wanted kids. But this also makes the reason for the sudden separation all the more painful: his new girlfriend is pregnant with twins. This is the absolute low point in my friend's life.

'I just want to get out,' Miriam weeps into the phone, 'just go somewhere for a year. But I've never been anywhere, except here in the Taunus region. Where could I possibly go?'

I can hardly hear her for all the sobbing, so I pull over. 'New York,' I tell her, and activate the car's hazard lights.

She stops crying. 'That's absurd. I can hardly speak English!'

'Then it's about time you learnt,' I answer, and I begin to

have a feeling, just an inkling, that in her case the 'absurd' might actually be just what she needs. As it happens, I'll be in Manhattan myself in ten days' time, visiting friends. So, who knows . . .

'Absolutely not! I thought you were going to make a clever suggestion,' she jabbers.

'Oh, come on, if you'd wanted to hear "Heligoland" you'd have called someone else.'

Probably true, she's probably thinking, because a few weeks later we're facing each other at JFK Airport in New York. I'm already in the Big Apple groove, with a decaf white mocha latte in hand. Miriam looks pale, has lost far too much weight, her eyes are large and shy. *If you can make it there you'll make it anywhere* it says in bold letters, a bit tritely, above the information stand where I'm waiting for her. Will Miriam 'make' it here? Right now, Sinatra seems light years away. 'Grit your teeth and go!' she says. This is our phrase for when the going gets rough. I put my arm around her and we head for the yellow cab queue.

That was eighteen years ago. Miriam is still in the USA. She founded an agency for expats in Brooklyn that helps Germans find their bearings in New York when they first arrive. Her call from the Taunus now seems like a fading snapshot from another life.

'If you'd supported me in my weakness back then, I'd probably still be sitting in Königstein, frustrated,' she once told me as we were sitting in Battery Park, looking out across the Hudson River, Lady Liberty sparkling in the distance. It's probably true. Sometimes it's good to make yourself thoroughly unpopular with friends by suggesting something that may seem insensitive at the time but has a healing effect in the long term. Reminding friends of who they are, when they've forgotten. Not telling them what they *want* to hear, but what they *have* to hear in order to regain their strength – a radical act of love that can really be helpful.

'I don't want to support you in your weakness.' A sentence applicable in many situations, and one that is sometimes better thought than said – occasionally, that does the trick too.

There was a time in my life when I had a reputation for being a walking information booth. It seemed to me like I was happily feeding info to the entire nation – tips, contacts, ideas. Looking back, it's hard for me to comprehend. But when the same person asked me for the fourth time if I could give him Ben's number I realized that something wasn't quite right: if I kept doing other people's work for them they would keep relying on me. It's only human. Instead of noting down numbers in their own contacts lists, it was more convenient to just peek into mine. Of course, you don't develop further by applying that principle. So, I freed myself from those entanglements, and I can tell you it was quite a task, dismantling the image I had unwittingly created of myself. 'I don't want to support you in your weakness' was a helpful thought during this time. But I rarely actually said it. It sounded a bit too brash, even if it accurately described the situation. But the milder version was well accepted and did the trick: 'It was a bad idea of mine to be directory enquiries. Please organize your contacts yourself from now on. This service is not available any more.' And, what do you know? Nobody asks me for Ben's number any more. It did have a positive side-effect, I suppose: I still know his number by heart. Hi Ben!

'Words show you how someone wants to be. Deeds show you how someone really is.' There's a lot of truth in that saying, as a client of mine from Vienna recently discovered.

He's on cloud nine the first time we meet. The conference rooms in his company are being renovated, so we're sitting on bright-yellow armchairs in an extremely colourful hotel lobby. He tells me he's in love with a new colleague of his. Since she entered his life, everything is suddenly rosy – la vie en rose! However, the next time we meet, things are far less rosy. The go-getter colleague, whom my client admired for her professional attitude at work, is a mess at home. 'The hallway was cluttered with shoes that had just been thrown there, and the floor of the apartment was littered with unpaid bills – it was just crazy!' he exclaims, nervously running his fingers through his hair.

'So, how did you react?'

'Well, eventually I just paid for the lot.'

'Seriously?'

'Yeah, I couldn't bear the sight of them!'

That's one way to handle things. And the woman actually thought this was wonderful – which isn't so wonderful for him, I think. What message is she getting from this impulsive intervention? Probably: 'Oh, marvellous! If I put things off long enough someone will come along and take care of everything.' I say to him: 'You certainly supported her weak point.'

He shakes his head and replies in that typical Viennese drawl, 'Ein Schaaaas' – meaning: what a total balls-up.

It's not always the case when we help someone that we're doing them a favour. I remember a fellow student at university who kept borrowing money from others. That went well for a couple of years, even though he didn't always repay his debts. He got by. Scrounging and getting by was the best he could do, because this system doesn't have a learning curve. If your experience is that others will always get you out of the lurch, obviously you won't see any need to be self-responsible. Put differently: if I sense that others feel responsible for my good fortune I'm not going to develop an interest in it myself. So, to all those who tend towards saviour syndrome: better to hold back with those well-intentioned impulses. Ask yourself, instead, what is it that I'm supporting – that person's strengths or their weaknesses?

To be clear, of course it's nice to be there for someone, a beacon of hope, a light in the darkness. We just ought to be careful that we're not being a candle, that we don't sacrifice ourselves. Candles give light by consuming themselves. So, in the end, it was bright for everyone but the candle is gone, used up. Some people have an incredibly hard time with this. They're so full of empathy, they don't realize when they're becoming accomplices to someone's misfortune. Through unreciprocated generosity we're helping to ensure that someone we care about ends up in a place that isn't good for them – mired in their weakness. This sentence is one of the few negatively worded sentences of this book: 'I *don't* want to support you in your weakness.' I've consciously formulated it this way, because in this instance it feels right.

WHAT THIS SENTENCE GIVES YOU

CALMNESS
RESPECT
SOLIDARITY

47

**YOU ALWAYS HAVE
A CHOICE**

What a sight! The generously dimensioned corner office has a picture-perfect view of Zurich in all its glory: the Grossmünster church towers over the old town, on the horizon the Alps have a vanilla-coloured glow, and before us lies the shimmering surface of Lake Zurich. This is the backdrop in front of which three investment bankers are going bonkers. Tomorrow, the most important deal of the year will be signed. They've worked for this for months, and now, shortly before reaching their goal, they've got the jitters, especially the most experienced man in the team – let's call him Chris.

Chris always seemed unshakeable, yet now he seems to be losing it. He's pacing up and down the office, leafing through documents, sitting down, jumping up again, energy going nowhere.

'Have you got ten minutes?' I ask him, after plucking up my courage – who wants to head into a tornado?

He looks at me, aghast. 'Can't you see what's going on here? DEADLINE! I don't *have* ten minutes! I'm *ten hours* short!'

On a bad day this would be like a punch to my gut but today I'm taking it in my stride. 'I completely understand what's going on. So, I'll ask again: have you got ten minutes? Not for *me*, for *yourself*. For *this*!' I motion towards the terrace and walk ahead. In moments like these, I feel blessed that I regularly attended improvisational theatre classes. It really does help you to stay cool-headed in a difficult situation. We've discussed the topic: don't take things personally. Remember?

Still incredulous, he actually does come out on to the terrace and takes a few deep breaths.

'The way I see it, you're going crazy right now,' I venture. Better just keep talking. 'By which I mean, you're *beside* yourself. But in that state you're just wasting time. If you just trust me, we'll do an exercise now that will bring you back into your centre – I mean, seeing as you have important things to do.' He hasn't said anything yet. 'It'll cost you a few minutes and you'll probably gain two hours. Are you on board?'

This is where Chris bites the bullet: 'Let's do it.'

And so we stand there, in front of this grand alpine setting, doing breathing exercises that re-establish a balance between the left and right sides of the brain. Then I ask him to focus on the clouds in the sky above us. 'Study every little detail, as if your life depends upon it.' He seems fully committed, because three minutes later, when the little gong on my phone says 'time's up', he's looking much more relaxed and he does appear to be more centred.

'And that's it?' he asks sceptically, adjusting his glasses.

I explain to him the difference between linear time, which passes second by second, and qualitative time, in which everything seems to stand still – in the here and now. 'Visit this place regularly when you're feeling rushed and impatient. It's worth it.'

Chris nods. 'It's the only time that exists anyway,' he philosophizes, quite unexpectedly.

I'm surprised. How true.

We always have the choice to try desperately to 'catch up' with the time, or briefly step aside and remind ourselves of what really matters. Whether we spend half an hour when we're stuck in traffic nervously drumming our fingers on the steering wheel, singing along to the radio, or using the time productively for something else, the journey will still take as long as it takes. Whether we want to get flustered or stay calm, feel the need to be in the right, or simply let go – how we react to something is always up to us. Nobody forces us to get stressed out; we just tend to forget this little fact of life: 'You always have a choice.'

Some may think this sounds like a calendar motto, and argue: 'What about the really cruel strokes of fate?' Let's suppose a young woman loses her leg in an accident. I can hardly begin to imagine how terrible that must be, a totally life-changing experience. And still, there are many different ways of dealing with it. 'My life is pointless now, I'm going to take a load of sleeping pills and that'll be it.' That's one option. 'Who will want a relationship with me now?' someone else might think, and slide into depression. Yet another woman may feel the first fragile blossoming of happiness while she's doing rehabilitation exercises. She keeps going, and two years later she's taking part in the Paralympics. And there might even be a woman – let's call her Heather – who founds a charity after her accident, meets Paul McCartney, marries him, gets divorced six years later and settles for £24.3 million. What I'm saying is, there's plenty you can do with just one leg. And as simplistic as it may sound in this condensed form, it's not the missing leg that determines the direction, it's the head. And I'm pretty sure that when Heather Mills was lying in hospital after her accident she wasn't thinking: 'Right then, I'll marry Paul McCartney.'

'You always have a choice' was also Nelson Mandela's conviction during his twenty-seven years in solitary confinement – which certainly won't have struck him as a choice. For a person condemned to a life in prison who steps into a seven-by-nine-foot cell, even thinking such a thought is a huge achievement – even more so when you don't know that you'll 'only' spend twenty-seven years behind bars. I can think of a number of things someone in his situation *might* have thought or done. But, secretly writing books at night, always maintaining an inner outlook towards freedom, focusing on forgiveness and letting go of bitterness, being released and, four years later, becoming South Africa's first black president . . . I *couldn't* have imagined that. What a journey.

'How do I want to feel?' 'What do I want to think?' 'How do I want to behave?' Three questions Mandela probably asked himself regularly. And each of us, no matter what the circumstances, can choose our own answers to these questions. Nobody else has a say here. Many try to intervene, but we don't have to let them.

'I always have a choice – seriously?' your head might be thinking, while rolling out a whole battalion of counter-arguments: upbringing, background, character, belief system . . . No further questions, your honour, says the attorney for the left part of our brain after presenting this list of circumstantial evidence, unable to believe that it's possible to change our lives at any time. Despite trauma, terrible medical diagnoses, war or a cruel twist of fate – yes, it is possible. There are so many moving stories from people, amazing stories that give us hope and lift our spirits.

'You always have a choice.' The popular coach and author Laura Malina Seiler would most probably agree. For years she has enthusiastically encouraged people to practise for-giveness, self-love and appreciation. And she has been doing so with passion, humour and energy on all media, in podcasts, meditations, interviews, ceremonies, in her books and online courses. Hardly surprising that she touches so many people on an emotional level. Perhaps this book has enriched you with some new ideas too. There are so many ways to find inspiration.

'You always have a choice.' A joyful message to oneself, when we happen to have temporarily forgotten the word *or*. Do we want to be in the right, *or* happy? Do we want to think about a problem, *or* about the solution? Do you want to live in the future, *or* now? Asking himself this last ques-tion got the time-pressured Swiss banker I started this chapter with out of his quandary. Since then, whenever I see mountains, I can't help being reminded: 'You always have a choice.'

WHAT THIS SENTENCE GIVES YOU
RELIEF
FREEDOM
PROSPECTS

48

YOU'RE RIGHT

I've always found it fascinating that police officers and public order officials (yes, these exist in Germany – they work for the Ordnungsamt, or Order Office) can't just rejoice when parking offenders immediately confess to having broken the rules and agree to pay a fine. I mean, what *is* there to argue about? As a rule, no-parking signs or double lines are clearly visible, everyone knows what they're allowed and not allowed to do. So, it seems logical that if you break the rules you'd simply accept responsibility for doing so. Yet, when someone displays this attitude, it seems to frustrate the people whose job it is to distribute tickets or collect fines. 'We don't often get that,' a police officer once told me. He seemed almost a bit insulted that I didn't want to play the wicked-rulebreaker-versus-diligent-cop routine. Purse in hand, I had freely admitted that I'd broken the law. He didn't like it, wanted to lecture me, tried various approaches, and eventually gave up because he kept running into this wall of sincere agreement.

These officers are used to being dragged into a discussion. They expect you to put on a look of innocence and say: 'Reeeeally?! No parking? Ah, but I only wanted to dash into the flower shop. Where else could I have left the car?' All the while looking this way and that, eyes never connecting. Not my cup of tea.

Would law enforcement officers really prefer it if people who had passed their driving test didn't know the rules? Do they feel more sympathetic towards befuddled drivers than the ones who know what they're doing? Is quarrelling better than a willingness to accept responsibility? Since I'm a big fan of self-leadership and solution-oriented thinking, I find this hard to fathom, and when someone tries to lecture me I'll happily shorten proceedings by saying: 'You're right.' It's another one of these tiny sentences with a huge effect that people find hard to say, even though it's beautifully simple and brings miraculous results.

Most of us simply love to be in the right – that's perfectly natural. Who would ever, in an argument, say 'I hope I've got it wrong'? Of course we want to be right, and it has nothing to do with our personality, incidentally. It's just the way our brain is wired. After all, it has worked hard to piece together all those fragments of information life offers us so that we can hold opinions, and have the arguments to support them. The logical part of our brain obviously wants these causal chains to be flawless. And the ego is also constantly seeking approval. So, when others agree with us we immediately feel good and prick up our ears. 'You're right' heightens our attentiveness for everything that comes after these words.

You can also use this effective little duo as an emergency escape for arguments that have got out of hand, when you want to change course and head in a less turbulent direction. I discovered this once, by pure chance.

A cloudy November day in Munich. I'm sitting in one of those typical conference floors: long corridors displaying original paintings by promising artists, and doors leading into rooms that, for some reason, have been given the names of cities. Today I'm conducting a pitch training session in Oslo. I've just announced it's time for the lunch break – at last. My very eager client and I have been working solidly for four and a half hours. There's a lot at stake for him. To be promoted, he has to convince an international panel of his business plan, and of course he wants to look good. His first attempt, the previous year, failed, and there won't be a third chance. That's why I'm here. We've got a lot to get through, so we agreed to only have a half-hour break – which is a challenge in itself if you subtract the time to walk to the canteen, the wait for lifts and standing in the queue.

I'm hurrying to the cloakroom when a senior partner in the company, who I know from a sales workshop I gave, approaches me. 'Well, if this isn't a lucky coincidence. Fantastic, Ms Kuschik! You can come straight with me. We're just having a rehearsal with a senior sales manager who has to give a presentation next week.' He leans towards me and conspiratorially lowers his voice. 'She's dreadful. Worse than dreadful! Of course, we can't tell her that, but she desperately needs professional coaching, and that's why we briefly require your services.'

Um . . . briefly?! This is where my instinct tells me to

grab my coat and head for the lift. It's bound to fail. A nervous woman being put under pressure, who probably realizes she can't be at her best under these conditions and senses that the partners are unhappy, but she's not being told so . . . This woman is supposed to subject herself to a crash course, without any confidence-building measures, delivered by a stranger who pops up out of nowhere and shows her a few magic tricks that are meant to instantly transform her into a presentational genius? Um . . . let me think . . . no! Not really doable.

So I haven't got a clue why I agreed to do it. Perhaps my ego loved the idea of winning against the odds. Perhaps I wasn't very good at saying 'no' yet. In any event, I accepted the challenge, even though it felt wrong. And, of course, it could only go wrong.

I do my best, take shortcuts where possible, engage and encourage her. Yet I also need to be crystal clear and to-the-point, and it all gets to be too much for the poor soul; she was already almost in tears when I entered the room. It must have felt to her as if she was being hijacked. And her bosses in the background, bellowing 'That's it! Well said! Otherwise it'll fail!' every time I said anything, probably didn't help either. While I'm desperately trying to figure out what to do, things turn really sour. The woman starts to cry and the senior partners suddenly change sides. 'No, you really can't say it in such a crass way, Ms Kuschik!' they complain, citing precisely the tips they'd applauded a moment before. 'Look, you've really upset Rosa!'

I'm angry. Really angry. Because, in spite of everything, they're right. I'm angry with myself, because I allowed them to drag me into this farce. Because I didn't trust my intuition. Because giving it your best and not achieving anything at all is a miserable combination. Because I really understood this woman and would have liked to give her the time she needed. Because the game her bosses were playing with her was so transparently dishonest. And, because now I would have to wait until 7 p.m. to get something to eat.

'You're right,' I suddenly hear the autopilot inside me say – a neat intervention at this late stage in the journey. Irritation all round, followed by silence. So, I continue: 'You're absolutely right. I definitely shouldn't have agreed to this. That was a totally unprofessional thing to do. I'm really sorry.'

Now, the first senior partner makes an interesting U-turn: 'No, no, Ms Kuschik, no need to blame yourself!'

'But I do,' I respond. 'You were right! It was pathetic of me to try and squeeze this in.'

Rosa stops crying, the men lighten up. 'It was an unfortunate situation, and we really did kind of ambush you,' one of them admits. 'And you did give some very helpful advice,' the second senior partner now chips in – and even Rosa is nodding her head. I'm shaking mine – in my thoughts. What an emotional rollercoaster experience, for everyone. And, luckily, I only just managed to slam on the emergency brake.

Since then, I've discovered that 'You're right' almost always does the trick. A real ear-catcher, it instantly calms tempers and instils a sense of goodwill – unless you're distributing parking tickets in Berlin. A two-word de-escalation enhancer. Above all, an effective straight-to-the-point tool for when you've forgotten to take yourself or others seriously. Apply this sentence generously, and appreciate the times when it's really true.

And if we happen to meet one day, feel free to tell me what these simple words 'You're right' have done for you.

WHAT THIS SENTENCE GIVES YOU

HARMONY
SELF-REFLECTION
CLARITY

When I give homework at the end of a workshop day, I'll sometimes purposely keep it quite general and hope no one notices. I'd rather everyone *thinks* they've understood the material; the learning curve during the next session can be much higher that way. Because one thing's clear: unfortunately, understanding alone doesn't pay off. Knowledge without practical experience is just theory. When we actually *apply* our knowledge it's a different matter. Of course, we all know this – otherwise, anyone would be able to drive a car after reading a book about it. Yet, strangely enough, when it comes to business training, and especially at management level, many seem to forget this fact. To compound matters, few participants allow themselves to acknowledge the new skills they've acquired; often, they're too busy trying to look good within the group and act as if they've known everything all along. Giving it a joyful 'Wow, that worked really well!' seems to be really hard, whereas a lethargic 'Well, it ain't that new – I knew most of it already' seems to be an easier response. The good thing is, the truth soon becomes apparent.

A treehouse colony under snow-capped fir trees, somewhere in the woods between Geneva and Lausanne in French Switzerland. A fantastic place to really switch off. I have managed to persuade the senior team in the company that commissioned me that people are much more receptive off-site than in a company conference room where assistants are constantly sneaking in, trying to get documents signed. The willingness to learn new things is simply far greater in a fresh environment. So, here we are, in the middle of the forest, and at night each participant switches on the torch-function on their phones and climbs up the rope ladder into their treehouse. A whiff of adventure, with a high eco rating and glam-camp ambience. Two women, four men, all of them managers their company regard as high-potential – meaning it's happy to invest in them because they're already good, but they lack that certain je ne sais quoi. 'Assured Leadership' is the title of the course. Right now, we're evaluating the homework I gave them three weeks ago – the last time we were here. The topic back then was 'focused delegation'. Everyone said 'that's an easy one', and I had to restrain myself from giving a detailed explanation of the task.

Yet now it's quickly becoming clear that, despite the log-cabin charm and the gentle crackle from the fireplace, the mood is somewhat subdued, and only Suzanne is able to provide us with positive feedback. The others complain that their staff never listen, do the opposite of what they've been asked to do, and that delegating tasks is simply nerve-racking. They demand tools and effective tips – but that's not what I have on offer. Writing *Three Steps to Success* on the whiteboard isn't my style, and it doesn't work. Much better that they discover the steps for themselves by looking at how Suzanne's handled it. That way, things will click into place.

And it's fascinating: after twenty-three years' experience in leadership training I can report that things are as they always have been – people don't ask enough and talk too much. Fixed, regular team meetings provide a good example of this. Most managers will express exactly what they want, some quite forcefully. But then, they ask the wrong question: 'Is all that clear?' When the team members nod, the meeting ends and the inevitable confusion begins. Because, why do we nod when someone asks if everything is clear? We nod to confirm that we've understood what we've understood. And that's often something different from what the sender of the message intended. Added to which, the term 'clear' is, like so many things in life, a matter of interpretation and, therefore, subjective.

What Suzanne did differently from the others – and did very well – was the way she ended her meetings: 'So, listen up, everyone. Who of you is doing what exactly? Pierre, you start!'

'Quelle bonne idée!' I call out, delighted, and that's about as far as my French goes. 'That's the way, Suzanne!' A perfect closing, and pretty simple really. Because, if we let everyone say for themselves how they have understood their brief, this will be where misunderstandings can be intercepted and clarified.

Letting others repeat, in their own words, what they

understood considerably increases the chances of the message that was sent being received. And only then does the sentence heading this chapter make perfect sense: 'I'll take you at your word.'

You've probably sensed it: this sentence is a wriggle-room reducer. Once a commitment has entered the equation, there is a completely different energy from the one you get when people nod along to things. 'I'll take you at your word' confirms that someone has promised us something and committed to it – and everyone could hear it. A far superior leadership style.

'This is getting on my nerves,' one of the four men suddenly groans – his contribution to a hitherto inspiring discussion. 'We're supposed to lay it out for everyone? I already work twelve hours a day; now I'm supposed to be super-careful what I say, and when I say it. I'm fed up with having to deliver all the time. The others have to pull their weight too.'

I completely understand this reaction. In an ideal world, I'd also like to live on an island paradise somewhere where everyone shares my values. Greetings to cloud-cuckoo-land, but the world doesn't work that way. It's different. People are different. Yet, we have the opportunity to expand our knowledge, to become more tolerant, more empathic, more patient, or whatever it is we need to make our communication with others easier. And, in the final analysis, with ourselves as well.

Since the annoyed team member – let's call him Philip – is a big football fan, as became clear during our raclette dinner the night before, I say to him: 'Reaching your goals is basically like playing football, Philip. You don't run to where the ball is, but to where it will be – right? Same principle for everyday life.'

He shifts his head from side to side, weighing this up. Doesn't look like he agrees.

Leadership – one of the major themes in the business world and, consequently, often a focus of training. I think that *self*-leadership is far more important. Because, if we don't know how to govern our own thoughts, don't know how to steer our own feelings and behaviours, how are we supposed to guide others successfully? To my mind, self-leadership is the prerequisite for skilful and effective leadership of others.

Most people are greatly relieved when they realize that successful leadership doesn't mean *working even harder*, but rather *enabling others to work*. It's not about constantly serving up snack-sized bits of information, pre-emptively doing all the work yourself, allowing others to passively listen and nod. That's not good leadership, and people don't learn anything. Assured leadership is a four-step process: asking questions, delegating, getting a commitment, and then – very important – letting go. This way everyone can experience personal growth, including the person who's leading.

'Before we speak, we are the masters of our words. Once we have spoken, our words are our master' – a Thai proverb that fits quite neatly here. Words count for much more when we let others say them in their own way. And it's the only way we can take people at their word. Only then are words really worth something.

'I'll take you at your word' has a calming effect on those who say it, and it confers an obligation on those who hear it. A short sentence with which self-leadership and leadership can be more easily and naturally effective.

WHAT THIS SENTENCE GIVES YOU

COMMITMENT
CLARITY
STRENGTH

50

I'M GOING TO TAKE IT IN MY STRIDE

I love Thailand. The landscape, the mentality, the food, the massages, and the heat as well. But, on this day, it's so humid even the Thais seem a bit strained and are using anything that's flat and lightweight to fan themselves. Feeling lethargic, I'm pondering whether going for a swim in a sea which has a temperature of 89°F can seriously be considered *cooling down*. I could do with a tropical downpour – better still, a cold German one.

Just then, a Thai family, all very smartly dressed – apparently belonging to a wedding party – enters the terrace. While they're considering where to sit, a tourist with lobster-red sunburn on his back (and fully exposed to the sun, regardless) bangs a bottle of soy sauce on the table. Something seems to be stuck. The lid flies off and a gush of dark-brown sauce splashes on to the radiant-white sarong of the beautiful Thai woman standing directly beside him. 'My goodness!' the man intones, with a strong Saxonian dialect (think Gert Fröbe as Goldfinger in the classic Bond movie). 'Blast it!' he huffs, and attacks the woman's sarong with a serviette, unwittingly making an even bigger mess. After the initial shock, the woman lifts her hand to her ear to feel if the frangipani blossom is still in place. Then she smiles at the man and says: 'Mai pen rai!' It's OK, never mind.

That's the way it is in Thailand. No matter if you accidentally break a glass, bump into a tuk-tuk, or splash soy sauce all over the bride's daughter's dress, 'Mai pen rai' is like a national mantra. And not just because it's polite; it's a way of looking at life, a kind of social contract. It expresses this: whether it matters or not, we're not going to make a big deal out of it, because we've decided it's not that important. 'Mai pen rai, kha!' Translated into my world this means: 'I'm going to take it in my stride.'

In the Land of Smiles, as Thailand is sometimes called, you can experience how the principle of deciding for yourself whether and when you want to feel this or that way about something actually works. We can get upset, or we can allow things not to matter. 'You always have a choice', remember? Yet, whereas sentence 47 still requires us to weigh things up and choose between various alternatives, 'I'm going to take it in my stride' needs only one simple decision, forever valid. The sentence expresses a *fundamental* attitude to life. It says: 'I'd *generally* prefer to take things in my stride.' It's just that many people never strike this deal with themselves. So, it's little wonder we get agitated when the plans we've devised for our life don't always go . . . well, according to plan.

'I'm going to take it in my stride.' If we distilled this sentence into one word, that word would be 'equanimity'. In Buddhism, it's one of the four sublime states. Loving kindness, compassion and sympathetic joy are the others. The question is always: which energy do I want to accommodate? Fear, anger, equanimity, joy? It's for us to decide.

'It's reeeally difficult! I can't get my mind round it!' a client called Markus laments during a recent telephone coaching session.

'Everything's difficult before you can do it,' I answer, feeling quite Buddha-like, though it could also be a quote from my mum: when I was a child, she always said, 'If you never practise something, it's only logical you won't be able to do it. So, go practise!' Can't argue with that.

I remember sitting beside her for seven hours once, on a spread-out newspaper in front of the Eiffel Tower. Twice, after endless queuing, we try to get the lift to the top. The first time they tell us it's broken, and the second time, 'Nous fermons' (We're closing). We come back earlier the next day, convinced we'll make it this time. But where are these masses of people heading? That's right: to the Eiffel Tower. Turns out it's the national holiday and everyone has had the same idea.

The famous tower is in the hands of pyrotechnicians who are fixing batteries of rockets to the steel girders. 'Yeseh, zere will bee génial fireworks!' a French woman with a picnic basket enthuses as we crane our necks and gaze upwards, unsure what to do next. In the end we spend the entire Sunday here, sizzling in the sun, talking, playing games, watching people and laughing a lot – and I find myself wondering whether equanimity is inheritable. Then, in the evening, there's a goosebumps moment as thousands of people suddenly stand up and, hands on their hearts,

sing along to 'La Marseillaise'. Finally, of course, the pyro-
technics. I must say that the term 'génial' doesn't do justice
to this spectacle. It was the best fireworks display I've ever
seen. Merci.

I think that viewing experiences as a kind of daily test generally makes a lot of things easier. After all, we live life
looking forward, and only understand it by looking back.
We never know what's coming. So, just keep riding the next
wave, for as long as you can. Looking at life this way can be
liberating. Letting it happen, accepting, letting go – that's
generally a very good idea. Because, taking things in one's
stride has nothing to do with the number of problems we
have, or don't have. It's a choice, a decision.

Something has happened that you don't like, that's hurt
you, or has thrown you back? Something unfair, or mean?
You can judge it, complain, get angry. You also have the
choice not to react at all, because the answer is already
clear: no matter what happens, you're wise to take it in
your stride.

'If the price you pay is not to be at peace with yourself,
the price is too high', as I read somewhere. Another thought
that can help to keep us rooted. And it takes us all the way
back to our first sentence: 'I decide who pushes my buttons.' The English answer to the Thai 'Mai pen rai'.

Let's not permit small things to ruin our greater joy. If
someone splashes soy sauce on your white clothes, just
pause, breathe out, breathe in, and remember . . . *this* particular moment, here and now. Perhaps someone next to
you will splutter: 'What if that stain doesn't come out? If it

was me, I'd be really annoyed!' Then you can relax, see this moment in relation to your whole life and simply say: 'I'm going to take it in my stride.'

WHAT THIS SENTENCE GIVES YOU

CALMNESS
SELF-DETERMINATION
AN ABUNDANCE OF LIGHTNESS

An Appeal

So here we are! These are my Fifty Sentences That Make Life Easier. How lovely that you joined me for this journey. It's certainly taken us to a lot of different places. Did you find a sentence that particularly appealed to you? Or three, or thirty? It can be illuminating to look at this more closely: which are your favourites? Do they perhaps all have a similar theme? Appreciation, clarity, boundaries, self-leadership – those are the four compass points that play a role throughout this book.

If you happen to be thinking, 'Bingo! That one has my name engraved on it, I'll always remember that sentence,' I'll have to be a bit of a spoilsport, because the chances are that without going one step further that's not going to happen. I'm talking about implementation – that tricky territory that lies between knowledge and ability. The phrase 'knowledge is power' is only true when power is wielded – otherwise it's just theory. So, my appeal to you is this: try these sentences, experience their effects, be amazed by the reactions, and in so doing create better possibilities for yourself. In this way, the book can be a real treasure trove.

Use it or lose it – that's the message. If we don't use something we quickly forget it, especially when it comes to personal growth, because our brain, our ego and old habits put up quite a fight before letting something new enter the system, no matter how euphoric we may initially feel. There really are dissenting voices within us that are incredibly sceptical when something is supposed to be easy.

Three little words can be quite useful here: 'Just do it' – as in 'Make it happen!' or 'I'm going to take it in my stride' (see sentence 50). It has been a constant theme for me while writing this book, telling you about my Fifty Sentences. Simple formulas for profound effects, so that you can make your life easier without having to resort to complicated tools. Now, when it comes to 'just doing it', it's your turn. How you go about it is up to you. If you decide to compile a personal best-of list of sentences you'll really use – perfect.

'The value of an idea lies in its use,' my niece, Marie, once said. She's a lively Aquarius with a thousand ideas that tend to compete for her attention, so I'm not surprised this sentence appeals to her. I like it too, because the most frequent question I hear when I'm coaching someone is: 'And how am I going to put that into practice?' Progressing from wanting to doing something appears to be a giant leap for most people. Still, now we know how easy it is to jump off a ten-metre diving platform: one step is all it takes – remember? The question isn't 'How does jumping off work?' but rather 'How can I remind myself that I wanted to jump?' And for this, three steps are helpful.

First: decide

You find an idea attractive, a goal worth striving for? There are, nevertheless, two possibilities why you won't get there. Some people imagine that the path that leads them there will be too hard to navigate; they want to arrive somewhere *now*, so they simply stay where they are. Others think it'll be a piece of cake, and overestimate themselves: 'Nah, I don't need to decide anything – I'll remember anyway.' Understand something, and then always apply this knowledge? Hmm . . . it very rarely works that way. A determined and aware decision to do something is much more promising. Therefore: decide which sentences you want to use and settle on a memory aid. Perhaps a Post-it note, a note in your calendar, a card with your favourite sentence on a little wooden stand?

Second: make a contract

Seriously?! If you just struggled to make a decision, you might be tempted to throw in the towel right now. As in: you can overdo it, you know! I'd still advise you to do it. We all know what it's like: if you don't make a deal with yourself you run the risk of being like that person on New Year's Eve who boldly proclaims 'I'm going to shed five kilos by February!' and is lying on the couch with a double portion of tiramisu on January the third.

We're usually quick to sign things without even reading the small print, but when it comes to personal growth we'd rather not sign anything – that would make it too big, too official. And yet, with the experience of twenty-three years as a coach, I'll say this: people who make a solid promise to themselves, put it in writing, sign it, even set a penalty for veering off course, reach their goals faster. There's an old German proverb, 'wer schreibt, der bleibt' – very roughly translated: what you put on paper, you'll stick to later.

What could such a vow, a contract with yourself, look like? 'The next time I start to feel angry because I think someone's having a go at me, I'll remember my promise and either say to myself, or audibly to the other person: I won't take it personally. Then I'll just continue the conversation and stay self-assured.' And concerning the penalty, perhaps: 'If I realize afterwards that I did forget the sentence, I'll donate thirty pounds to the Society of Broken Promises, or I'll postpone watching my favourite series for two days.' Whatever the price you pay, it should be high enough to hurt a little, but small enough to handle. And, since I can already hear the cries of indignation, no, it's *not* supposed to be a punishment – on the contrary. The penalty stands for how seriously you take yourself. Thus, it's not a punishment but a measure of the value you ascribe to yourself.

Third: practice

Knowledge becomes ability when we've forgotten how it works. So, this last step is about *forming* a new habit. That's most easily achieved in times of peace – an old Apache proverb. You don't grab your bow and arrows when the enemy appears on the horizon. You learn things in a playful way, when little is at stake. That's true in our case as well. Because, we know how it is, at work and in everyday life: suddenly we're caught up in an unexpected situation and have to react extremely quickly. Therefore, better to practise in 'peacetime' than to wait for the next surprise attack when winning the battle may depend on a quick-witted response.

For your new attitude to have an impact when it really matters, it's best to practise it in everyday situations: at the cheese counter, at a party, at the checkout, in the gym, while talking to friends on the phone. You can say 'I don't think that's really my department' without someone attacking you first, or taking you for granted – you can drop that in in less challenging situations. 'I think I'll just take *this*' can be wonderfully deployed any time you're eating out. 'I decide who pushes my buttons' can be a quick decision while you're washing your hands. 'I've changed my mind', 'I don't know', 'I think this issue is yours' – most sentences can easily be practised when the stakes are low.

And if it doesn't all go smoothly to begin with? What if you start out euphorically and mess up? Then just forgive yourself and proceed as you always do in life: stand up, brush yourself down, carry on. Or say the Thai mantra, Mai pen rai – never mind. And another old proverb comes to mind: 'If you trip and fall, you'll pay more attention to the road.'

In all likelihood, everything will work really well, really quickly. After all, these sentences have a highly successful track record, and have helped thousands of people in a whole range of different situations. So, if you do encounter difficulties, the problem might lie with the tonality, the way you've said them. If the tone is too serious, too bossy, or it sounds like you're making a big deal out of it, you're likely to come across as excitable, or on edge. We want to achieve the opposite. Let the sentences sound natural, light and incidental, as if you're ordering a drink. 'I'll have a Coke, please' – that's how you want it to sound when you say 'I completely understand you, and I'd like something else.' Self-assuredness always sounds cool, calm and collected.

Maybe some of you will experience that miraculous phenomenon that often follows perfect preparation. You've got your arsenal of sentences all lined up and you're raring to use them, to brilliantly assert yourself. All you need is the right situation, and then . . . it never comes. Weeks go by, months. And maybe that opportunity will never arise. If that's the case: congratulations! You have every reason to rejoice. Sometimes, when a new thought instantly penetrates deep into your system, it can actually change your aura, your attitude, your stance, and the way you're perceived. And once you have a new attitude, you obviously don't need the sentence any more, or a situation in which you could practise it. It really is amazing: as soon as we've found an answer, life changes the question.

And now? I'm curious to know what you're going to do with all these sentences, whether my stories inspired you, gave you insights or outlooks. And how eager you are to use some of these in your life. Because, naturally, that's always the greatest joy: creating lots of magical moments that make life easier. Let yourself be surprised by the effect your favourite sentences will have, sentences that have become so dear to me. I'm sending them into the world, and as I do so I'm thinking of that Banksy mural *Girl with Balloon*; as though I was climbing up on to the roof of my

Berlin apartment on this sunny Sunday, clutching fifty precious balloons. And I'm about to let them go.

My arm's raised to the sky. And I'm amazed to see them fly.

WHAT THIS BOOK GIVES YOU

FREEDOM

SELF-DETERMINATION

CONFIDENCE

Acknowledgements

Ben Posener – Translating a book about language is always tricky. If it's by an author who is a stickler for detail and is fond of stylistic quirks that are almost impossible to translate, the task is doubly difficult. I could only think of one person for the job: Ben Posener. Ben, you know me and you know both cultures so well. You're familiar with the world of coaching, and you understand the spirit of my words – as well as those crazy little sub-tones. You're excellent in both languages, yet you wanted to be persuaded. I'm so glad you were. This book, as it is, would not exist without you.

Laura Malina Seiler – You generous and wonderful person! You just casually cast an email into the universe, reached two people, and in doing so have now reached so many. Thank you, dear Laura, for your kind-hearted and abundant inspiration. Exceptional!

Ricarda Saul – Is there anyone in the publishing world who is more appreciative, smarter and benevolent than you? Thank you for your boundless enthusiasm and unwavering trust. I want to name an adjective after you. Right now.

Thimon von Berlepsch – Thank you for your recommendation, my dear, which, after all, is how it all began. Thank you for the miraculous connection we've had over so many years, and for your unconditional willingness to share.

Hermann Scherer – Mr Superlative. Who knows what I'd have done if you hadn't shouted 'This is a book!' after every fifth sentence. From afar, feeling close and grateful to you.

Sonja Ziemer – I'll always remember you kneeling in front of that wall, in wonderment. It's you who chose this book! A thousand thanks to you, my Sonne, my sunshine, my shining and confident treasure hunter! Schatzi and Patzi for ever.

Sarah Gräfensteiner – The things we've experienced together, my dear! And when the world was on pause, there you were again, as if you'd never been away. And, instantly, you knew what was going on. Thank you for being the ever-understanding Sarah. Family feeling.

Mum – For decades you always kept your fingers crossed for me, believed in me and were happy for me. Thank you, Mum! Without you, I wouldn't be here, you joyful, young Leipziger Räbchen, you.

Alex – Thank you for your enthusiasm and joyfulness while I was still silent. Thank you for the marvellous radiance and unshakable optimism which sustains you and the world around you and which always deeply touched me.

Annelie – You fiercely determined one! You just march into the station. And then, that evening when you unexpectedly left with the words 'Sooo, then you might as well start straight away!' That's total devotion. That's uniquely you!

Ben – You were so incredibly certain. Right from the start. You believed I could move mountains, again and again. And you were right. Thank you dearly, my friend. From the girl . . . well, you know what kinda eyes she got.

Egor – Thank you for your boundless generosity during the final phase. And how lovely that we share this weird sense of humour that always brings lightness and relief, even in the midst of the greatest chaos.

Florian – You loyal walker-and-talker, my ironic key-word server. Three of your spirited metaphors have found their way into this book. Have you discovered them yet?

Jens – What a gift, back then, that you took my yearning to be creative seriously – just like that – and jumped in for me. Incredible. I am forever grateful.

Kai – The number of times I listened to our brilliant mantra while writing . . . you fabulous artist! Thank you for accompanying me on this journey, from my roller-skate accident right up until now. Amazing.

Katrin – Eighteen thousand steps more, per week! Many thanks for your endless patience in sorting out the empire and for handing me bananas along the way.

Marco – Thank you for always being there, supporting me with your presence and devoted attention. My loyal friend. Everyone should have a Marco! Sometime I'll get round to printing that T-shirt.

Mimmy – When you left the island I got started. What to do with all that fabulous energy, all that love? Thank you for everything I learnt from you, my dear. You have enriched me.

Mitsch – Your heart is so big and so beautiful, and your trust. You were always there. Have always seen me as I am. Always listened. Tanti baci, bella mia. How wonderful that you exist!

Sarah – You were my anticipatory enthusiast. The things we experienced together! From plus one to client, to assistant, to coach, to bride, to always reliable friend. Fantastic!

Tania Maria – I'm glad I can only sense how much you really know – otherwise it would have knocked me off my feet a long time ago. Thank you for your wisdom, your patience, your incredible timing and your humorous depth. I'll just say: Boooook!

A heartfelt thanks to all the many wonderful corporate clients. I've learnt so much from your feedback and have grown fond of many of you. Special thanks to Eran Davidson, Matthias Frik, Ulrike Hasbargen, Marcus Höfl, Susanne Jäger, Katja Kahl, Conny Keller, Amelie Kern, Roman Köhne, Markus Link, Marko Müller, Christoph Schenk, Philipp Turowski, and also, clearly in my memory, Mark Smith. I had magic moments with all of you, and you were a valuable mirror to me. Thank you for your trust. I'm so glad you're all here!

Notes

Sentence 3: I apologize
Ben Furman, *It's Never Too Late to Have a Happy Childhood*
(BT Press, 1998). It is one of the greatest books ever published
in the field of psychotherapy.

Sentence 9: I think I'd better forgive myself
EDxTM (Energy Diagnostic and Treatment Method) is a
bioenergetic coaching and therapy method based on the
idea that psychological problems, such as those involving anxiety,
are linked to energy blockages in the meridian system. It is
based on the teachings of US psychologist Dr Fred Gallo.

Sentence 13: I'm not sure what this means
Paul Watzlawick (1921–2007) was an Austrian-American
philosopher, psychotherapist and communication theorist. Paul
Watzlawick, *The Situation Is Hopeless, But Not Serious: The Pursuit of
Unhappiness* (W. W. Norton & Company, 1983).

Sentence 15: When you point a finger at someone, you're pointing three at yourself
Friedemann Schulz von Thun's model has been variously named:
four-sides model, four-ears model, communication square. It was
first described in his book *Miteinander Reden*, volume 1 (Rowohlt
Taschenbuch Verlag, 1981).

Sentence 16: I can't afford not to
Bronnie Ware is an Australian author and songwriter. Her book
*The Top Five Regrets of the Dying – A Life Transformed by the Dearly
Departing* (Hay House, 2011) went from being a feature on a blog
to world bestseller in a short space of time.

Sentence 23: I'm sorry if I gave you the impression you could talk to me like that
'I'm just preparing my impromptu remarks' – quote from
Sir Winston Leonard Spencer Churchill, author, Nobel Prize
winner in Literature, and two-time British Prime Minister.

Sentence 25: I don't want to spend time on this
David Allen has written several internationally renowned
books on time management, the best known of which is
Getting Things Done: The Art of Stress-Free Productivity
(Penguin Books, 2001).

Sentence 42: I won't take it personally
Many of the names in this book are pseudonyms, but Kara
Johnstad is the real name of an amazing singer. She gives daily
singing lessons in her School of Voice in the Berlin district of
Zehlendorf (https://karajohnstad.com).

Sentence 45: I don't know how to, so I'll just give it a go
Sabin Tambrea interviewed on NDR Talk Show, 12 March
2021 (https://www.youtube.com/watch?v=e5j6ff51gxM).
Petra Bock, *Mindfuck – How to Overcome Mental Self-Sabotage*
(Knaur, 2011).

Sentence 47: You always have a choice

Laura Malina Seiler is a bestselling German author, life coach, speaker and producer. With her #1 podcast *happy, holy & confident* she has inspired a modern spiritual movement in Germany (https://lauraseiler.com).

FREE MEDITATION EXCLUSIVELY FOR READERS

For anyone keen to have a mental boost, this guided meditation offers powerful support. Close your eyes, prick up your ears and connect easily with your inner sense of self-confidence.

MY GIFT TO YOU!

MEDITATION

Notes

NOTES

NOTES

NOTES

NOTES

NOTES

NOTES

....

....

....

....

....

....

....

....

....

....

....

....

....

....

....

....

....

....

NOTES

NOTES

NOTES

....
....
....
....
....
....
....
....
....
....
....
....
....
....
....
....
....
....
....

NOTES

NOTES

About the Author

Karin Kuschik began her career as a songwriter and radio presenter before becoming a performance coach for business decision-makers and media celebrities, and a keynote speaker. She is committed to supporting people to be the best versions of themselves, and in *50 Sentences that Make Life Easier* – a number-one bestseller in Germany – she makes her expertise accessible to everyone for the first time. She lives in Berlin.